Illustrator:
Wendy Chang

Editor:
Evan D. Forbes, M.S. Ed.

Managing Editor:
Elizabeth Morris, Ph. D.

Editor in Chief:
Sharon Coan, M.S. Ed.

Art Director:
Elayne Roberts

Art Coordination Assistant:
Cheri Macoubrie Wilson

Cover Artists:
Tina DeLeon
Larry Bauer

Product Manager:
Phil Garcia

Imaging:
Evan D. Forbes, M.S. Ed.

INTI
ACTIVITIES FOR SOCIAL STUDIES

INTERMEDIATE

Author:
Kathleen Kopp, M.S. Ed.

Publishers:
Rachelle Cracchiolo, M.S. Ed.
Mary Dupuy Smith, M.S. Ed.

Teacher Created Materials, Inc.
6421 Industry Way
Westminster, CA 92683
ISBN-1-557690-404-0

TABLE OF CONTENTS

TABLE OF CONTENTS *(cont.)*

AN INTRODUCTION TO THE INTERNET

What Is the Internet?

Much of today's correspondence is done electronically; e-mail, fax, computer databases, and so on can be sent and information retrieved efficiently with the use of a computer or other technologically advanced machine. The Internet provides information resources through the use of a network specifically designed for computers. The slice of information from the Internet viewed as text and graphics is called the World Wide Web. Other pieces of the Internet include bulletin board systems, chat rooms, and e-mail services. Internet users can browse Web sites for information, order tickets, ask questions of an expert, accomplish virtually anything one can imagine, all without having to get out from behind a desk. This "information superhighway" takes Internet users virtually anywhere they want to go at any time. Travel to Alaska. Want to see the real thing? Book yourself a cruise!

The Internet is nothing more than a network of interconnected electronic data that crisscrosses and zigzags over miles and miles of phone line, creating a "Web." After identifying a particular topic, one may access Web sites available on the Internet. These Web sites may be independent of one another or connect to related Web pages. Textual links are usually a different color than the Web site's normal text. They may be purple or red words embedded in black text, for example. By clicking them, the Web page currently showing connects to the next link. Links can also be graphic items (pictures). Any time the cursor changes to a pointing hand, you know you've found a link.

How Do I Get There?

In order to explore the Internet, you will need four things: (1) a computer with Internet capabilities, (2) access to a network via a telephone line (an Internet service provider), (3) a Web browser such as *Netscape* or *Microsoft Internet Explorer*, and (4) a destination. Some online services, such as America Online and Compuserve, offer a network and Web browser all in one. This means that by launching the Internet icon, users automatically dial in to their network and view the Internet through their browser. Trouble may arise if you live in a remote area where there are no local access numbers to dial. So then not only are you paying the company for the use of its program, you also need to pay long distance telephone fees every time you log on. Many smaller (but local) Internet service providers have emerged to save Internet users huge phone bills. Check your local telephone directory and call (yes, with an actual telephone!) to set up access through a local Internet service provider's number. So far, these companies have been rather reasonable with their rates. You usually have a choice of limiting the amount of calling you may do, therefore limiting your Internet exploration time, or signing up for unlimited hours. This might be an option if you are considering downloading information and/or programs off the Internet, which can sometimes take hours, depending on the size of the program. Check out what's available to you in your area, and then decide which method of logging on and browsing is right for you.

AN INTRODUCTION TO THE INTERNET *(cont.)*

So Many Destinations, So Little Time

Once you're safely logged on, the virtual world is at your fingertips! This can be a blessing or a curse. Once you start exploring on the Information superhighway, you will find that some roads are endless while others run into a dead end. Some are toll roads and others are bridges. Don't be discouraged your first time on the Internet. If you make a wrong turn or end up in a deserted town, get back in that vehicle and keep on truckin'!

Take some time to just explore without a destination in mind. Get a feel for how the Web system works. Then try hunting for specific information on a particular subject. A host of popular search engines exist, such as Excite, Yahoo!, and Infoseek to name a few. Type in a topic of interest and search it. The computer will access any and all sites and related categories that match the topic. You may find a need to narrow a search by typing in more specific information or broaden the search by typing in a more general subject.

Most search engine home pages list popular subject areas, or categories, with which to begin a search. Try one of these headings and see where it takes you. If it's not what you're looking for, you can always abort this mission and return to the home page. (An icon specifically for this task, labeled <**Back**>, is at the top of the task bar.)

You've seen the advertisements for a company's Web site: http://www.[blah].com. This is called a URL or Uniform Resource Locator. Typing in an Internet address at the top of the task bar and striking the return key will launch you directly to that site.

Can I Ever Get Back?

You may find yourself easily lost if following a site that links and links to related topics. Make a bookmark of the site's home page before going on so that if you do make a wrong turn but want to keep exploring this site, you won't have to go back ten links to find the original page.

One may presume that no one has ever disappeared while exploring the Internet. It's not the Bermuda Triangle, although it may seem so to new users. A more accurate metaphor is an expanse of quicksand. When you first jump in, you're still fairly safe. But the more you move around and the deeper you get, the more difficult it is to escape. Fortunately, a safety line is always near.

The Internet works like any other computer program. When you're ready to quit, simply exit or quit the program. If you're online with a network separate from your browser, be sure to disconnect the phone connection. If you forget, the computer will stay "online" even though you're off to the grocery store. And this will use up valuable time with the Internet service provider while blocking the phone line to incoming (and outgoing) calls.

USING THIS BOOK

In this guide is a listing of sites related to specific topics which may be part of or supplement an intermediate social studies curriculum. Students will need to access a particular Web site to attain information to complete the activities.

Be sure to access the focus Web site (or destination URL) before engaging students in the activity. Web sites tend to change over time, and you don't want to meet with any surprises while browsing live with the class. If for some reason the Web site listed is no longer available, try one of the alternate URLs. Many of the focus sites in this guide are actually links or links within links of a home page. An arrow or icon may be at the bottom indicating "Go Back." If interested, link to view the original site of the focus Web site. But once again, be sure to preview it before viewing with the class.

Read over the steps to become familiar with the students' responsibilities for each task. See "Classroom Management Tips" on page 7 for more details on how to go about engaging all the students in active Internet learning.

Begin the lesson with the suggested pre-Internet activity. Access the destination URL, and be prepared to help the students obtain information as they participate in this high-tech manner of research. After the students have completed their online investigation and Internet activity, try one or all of the "Extended Activities" designed to supplement the focus activity.*

Students will need about 20 to 30 minutes to complete the actual online activity. Plan to spend additional time preparing or reviewing with the class during the pre-Internet and extended activities.

The focus Web sites were chosen because of their age-level appropriateness for intermediate students. Still, some of the textual information may be too difficult for some students to read independently. Students may need assistance when reading the text.

None of the activities calls for e-mailing or visiting a chat group. E-mailing takes a day or two. E-mailers send a message, and then the person who received the message responds. You may wish to e-mail the author or company responsible for a particular Web site to tell him or her how much the class enjoyed it, what they learned, etc. Chat groups are an instantaneous transfer of typed messages. Since you cannot control what others may write and, thus, what the students may read, this act of information exchange is not recommended. There are plenty of honest, wholesome, kid-related chat groups out there, but this guide is intended to help students use the Internet to gather information, not to chat with persons they have never met.

***Author's Note:** The materials list does not include supplies for the extended lessons.

Classroom Management Tips

The activities in this guide assume that the students have one computer in their classroom with Internet access. Incorporate the use of the Internet to ensure that all students have equitable experience on the Net in one of several ways. Some of the activities have instructions to launch the focus Web site as a class. Others suggest grouping the students and allowing them to take turns. Regardless of the instructions set forth in the individual activities, make a reasonable choice regarding this organizational strategy to suit the needs of your classroom.

To Launch a URL with the Whole Class

If this is the method of choice or if the activity calls for this, try attaching an overhead projector or television monitor to the computer if it has these capabilities. This will allow for easier viewing by the entire class. Make sure all the students have a copy of the activity page so they may follow along. Keep everyone on task by rotating volunteers to click at the site and read portions of the information.

Working in Groups

Another option is to have the students work in small groups to access the desired Web page(s). First provide a whole-class lesson demonstrating how to accomplish this. For occasions when you may not be directly available, elicit the help of an adult volunteer to make sure the students are typing in the exact URL, following the directions on the activity sheet, attaining the information necessary for successful completion of the activity, and avoiding the temptation of downloading or e-mailing. Volunteers may be co-workers, parent volunteers, administrators, or perhaps a school media specialist or technology teacher. Even if some students have prior experience using the Internet, be sure to provide them with the support they may need to successfully read the information and complete the activity pages.

One way to manage Internet groups effectively is to have the Internet activity be a center rotation. This way, all the students are engaged in a meaningful project while you help those on the Internet. And all the groups will have a turn on the Internet.

Save It for Later!

A final option is to save the sites for easier access, unless the students are to practice typing in the exact URL. (See “Internet Tips” on page 9 for information about *WebWhacker*, bookmarking, and saving the file.)

INTERNET TIPS

- Know the exact URL or have a specific topic in mind to investigate.
- Type in the EXACT Uniform Resource Locator (http://). This includes all letters, numbers, punctuation, and symbols. Just like an address, sending a package to the wrong door will result in a "return to sender" message or someone else enjoying your visit.
- Typing in a series of words to search will instruct the computer to link all those words individually. Put quotation marks around the words that act as one topic (e.g., "Native Americans" or "United States Geography").
- Be patient when downloading sites with bountiful graphics. These take up a lot of computer memory. Large graphics may take some time to fully "develop," depending on the speed of the modem and other uncontrollable factors. Try visiting the site and connecting to all the links prior to engaging the class. If the site is returned to within a reasonable amount of time, the computer will have held some graphic information in memory. This will accelerate the downloading time.

- Many persons or organizations with Web sites have encouraged businesses to advertise on their page(s). Be on the lookout for links to advertisements and learn to ignore them (unless they are promoting something in which you may have an interest). Teach students to do the same. If you accidentally link to an advertisement, click the <**Back**> arrow at the top of the task bar to return to the previous page.
- Text portions of Web sites usually arrive much quicker than accompanying graphics. Arrow down the page and read the text while the graphics are downloading. Then arrow back up the page and view the artwork and pictures.
- Murphy's Law definitely applies anytime you wish to incorporate technology into the classroom. Expect things to go wrong, even after careful planning. If a Web site is unavailable or your ISP line is busy, have an alternate project ready for the students to complete. If the computer displays a "return to sender" message, double-check to be sure you typed in the exact URL.

INTERNET TIPS *(cont.)*

- A relatively new software program called *WebWhacker* is ideal for classroom surfing. This program allows users to download an entire Web site onto the hard drive or zip drive. Users may also select the number of levels (or links) to include. Then the students need only launch the file name of the saved information to complete the activities. Although students won't actually be "on the Net," the information is viewed as if they really were, and their interaction is censored by guaranteeing they can't e-mail or download programs.
- Another option is to bookmark the sites. (Click **<Bookmark>** from the task bar and drag down to **<Add a Bookmark>**.) When students go online, they only need to click and drag to the correct bookmark; they will automatically be transported to the focus Web site.
- Another way to save sites is by selecting **<File. . . Save As>**. Choose a drive to save the site and give it an appropriate filename. A word of caution, though: Saving Web sites will only save the text portions (no graphics), and some sites won't save at all. (They look like computer script when the file is opened.) A final option is to simply print the site.
- The information age is here to stay (at least for a while), but some parents may be uncomfortable with their children's access to the Internet. Before beginning any Internet projects, have parents sign the consent form on page 140.
- Check out ALL Web sites before allowing students to go online. Although the Web sites in this guide were consulted beforehand, some sites may have changed, been moved, or somehow incorporated information not appropriate for young students. If this is the case, do some investigative research on your own to find a suitable Web page for the class. Some reliable and user-friendly search engines are listed on the following page.
- Have a question about a site? Click on FAQ (frequently asked questions) to see if others have thought the same thing. If your question isn't spotlighted at this link, at least you'll learn information you hadn't thought to ask. E-mail the creator of a site to beg the answers to the most burning questions or to express your thanks for providing a fine educational Internet opportunity for students. Most creators are quick with their responses; they usually write back by the next day.

TO SAVE WEB SITES

- Use a *WebWhacker* program
- Bookmark the site
- Save it as a regular document
- Print it

SEARCH ENGINES AND SOCIAL STUDIES KID LINKS

Search Engines

Try these to research a specific topic of interest.

Alta Vista
http://www.altavista.com/

Excite
http://www.excite.com/

Infoseek Guide
http://guide.infoseek.com/NS

Kids World 2000
http://www.ecst.csuchico.edu/~bigkid/kidsworldindex.html

Yahoo!
http://www.yahoo.com

Yahooligans!
http://www.yahooligans.com

Social Studies Kid Links

These sites offer links to topics of children's interests.

Biographical Dictionary
ftp://obi.std.com/obi/Biographical/

Britannica Online
http://www.eb.com

Discovery Online: History
http://www.discovery.com/area/history/history.html

The History Channel
http://www.historychannel.com/

National Geographic World Online
http://www.nationalgeographic.com/media/world

A VIRTUAL TOUR OF THE INTERNET: PIRATES

Objective:

Avoid a mutiny by introducing your mateys to the Internet with a focus on pirates. Students first learn to use a search engine as a guide to a desired destination. Then they apply their Internet skills to complete an Internet-dependent activity about pirates.

Materials Needed:

- chalkboard
- one copy of page 13 for each student
- one copy of page 14 for each student

Focus Web Sites—Destination URLs:

Yahooligans!
http://www.yahooligans.com

History of Piracy
http://www.filmzone.com/cutthroat/highseas/highseas.html

About This Site: Read up on the most famous **Rogues**, the **Punishments** they inflicted, and the yummy **Victuals** they partook of at this historic site about pirates.

Alternative Web Sites:

Pirates! by National Geographic.com/Kids
http://www.nationalgeographic.com/features/97/pirates/maina.html

Land Pirate's Pirate Page
http://www.concentric.net/~Chrilena/

Blackbeard!
http://ocracoke-nc.com/blackbeard/

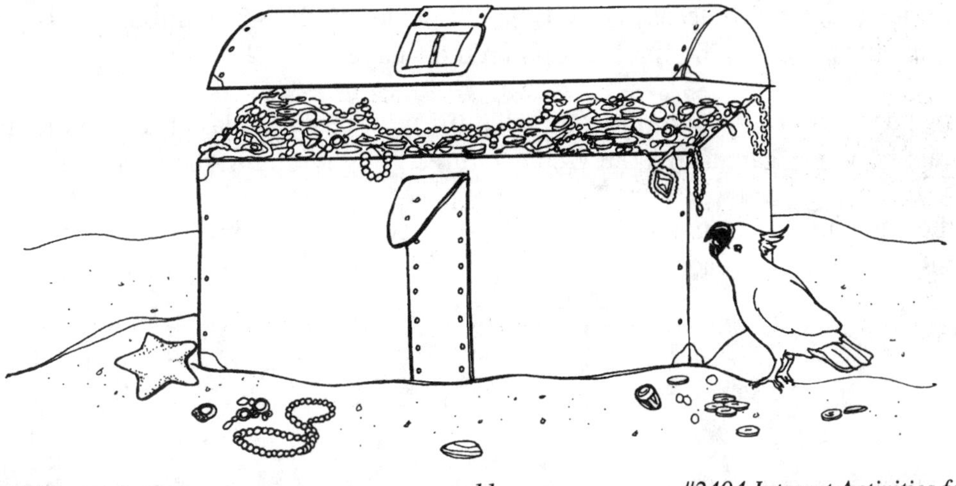

A VIRTUAL TOUR OF THE INTERNET: PIRATES *(cont.)*

Pre-Internet Activity:

Don a patch, bandanna, and hooked arm (if possible) to introduce this activity. Make a list of all the actions of pirates that the students know of on the chalkboard. Review the list when the students are done brainstorming. Would they say that pirates were friendly, considerate fellows? Why or why not? Then ask them if they know the differences among a pirate, privateer, and buccaneer. Tell the class that they will learn this and many more facts when they visit an Internet site that tells all about pirates.

Teaching the Lesson:

1. Review these Internet vocabulary words with students. (Refer to the "Glossary of Internet Terms" at the end of this guide to explain words with which you may be unfamiliar.) They will need to know what the words mean when they take their tour.
    - log on
    - Internet
    - search engine
    - URL
2. Distribute a copy of "Touring the Internet," page 13, to each student. Read through it with the class so they will be familiar with how to research using a search engine. To aid them in their tour, help them follow the directions on the activity page as a class.
3. Review the Web site. Discuss some possible reasons to explain why this person constructed this Web site (number 5 on page 13).
4. Link to read about the **Rogues** with the class. As they read, students complete this section on their answer sheet. With each link, demonstrate how to use the <**Back**> arrow from the task bar to link back to the previous Web page.
5. Then link to **Punishments**. Help clarify any punishments the students may not understand. Then they complete this section of their answer sheet.
6. The final link students will access is **Victuals**. Read about the scrumptious meals pirates enjoyed; then the students complete the final section on their page.
7. After the students have successfully completed the tour, take the class back on the Internet and demonstrate how they can access the Web site directly by typing in the destination URL.
8. Review the students' list from the pre-Internet activity. What additional information can they add? Has the information they read at this Web site changed their opinions about pirates? Discuss.

TOURING THE INTERNET

Name ____

Directions: Read and follow the directions below to learn how to search on the Internet and find a site that will tell you about pirates.

1. Have your teacher log onto the Internet. *Yahooligans!* is a popular search engine for students. To access this search engine, find the **Location** box at the top of the screen and type in this URL:

   http://www.yahooligans.com

2. Now you are at the *Yahooligans!* home page. Read the list of sites from which you may choose. Move the cursor around the colored words. Notice how it changes from a cursor to a pointing hand. Any words or pictures on the Internet that change to a pointing hand are links to another site. To find information about a particular subject, you need to tell *Yahooligans!* what kinds of sites to look for. Click in the search box. A blinking cursor appears. Type in the word **pirates** and click <**Search**>.

3. A list of related categories and direct links appears. Look at this category link:

   Around the World: U.S. States: Pennsylvania: Sports and Recreation: Pittsburgh Pirates

If you click this, you will see a list of sites that have to do with all of these categories.

4. Click on the category **Around the World: History: Pirates**. A list of pirate sites appears. Choose the one with the title **History of Piracy**. The URL at the top of the page changes to

   http://www.filmzone.com/cutthroat/highseas/highseas.html

5. Think about why this site was created. The first link you need to access is the one that tells about **Rogues**. Read the information here to complete the first section of the student page, then continue to follow the links.

PIRATES OF THE CARIBBEAN

Name ____

Launch this Web site: http://www.filmzone.com/cutthroat/highseas/highseas.html

Directions: Follow the links at this Web site to answer the questions.

Click on the **Rogues** link. Read about Blackbeard and Black Bart. Write their real names under their faces. Add to their wardrobes to show how they dressed. Draw a line to the pirate responsible for the Jolly Roger.

____________________ ____________________

Click the **<Back>** arrow from the task bar. Now click on the **Punishments** link. Read the information and answer the questions.

1. Describe a cat-o'-nine-tails. ____
____
2. Tell what is was used for. ____
3. Who used it? ____
4. List three other punishments pirates used. ____
____

Arrow **<Back>**. Choose the **Victuals** link. Read about a pirate's menu. Draw a picture of his meal on the backside of this paper.

A VIRTUAL TOUR OF THE INTERNET: PIRATES *(cont.)*

Extended Activities:

- (Arrange ahead of time for a teacher of a younger grade to tell his or her class that some pirates are on the loose and they should take care not to get captured!) Discuss what the students learned about the Jolly Roger. (It warned others that the ship was plagued to keep prying eyes away, to prepare for battle, and to signal that no quarter would be given; "Old Roger" came to mean the Devil, a "Roger" or begging vagabond and was a slang term for a sea vagrant.) If desired, view some **Images** of **Jacks (Flags)** of pirates. Have the students design a flag as if they were pirates. Send students a few at a time bearing their colors to each "capture" a younger student from the class with which you arranged this ahead of time. They bring them back to class, read a short pirate or ocean story with them, and then return them to their proper teacher.
- Students may practice their coordinate skills with this buried treasure activity. Provide each student with two sheets of inch graph paper. They number the lines along the left side and bottom of the pages. Then they pick seven coordinates on one of the sheets to "bury" treasure by drawing small symbols for the treasure at those coordinates. Students pair off to play. Each student, in turn, calls out a set of coordinates. His or her partner tells if it's a hit or miss. The student marks the hits and misses on the blank sheet so he/she remembers which coordinates have already been called. Then the partner has a turn and does the same. The game is won when one partner uncovers all seven treasures from his or her partner's map.
- Before the students arrive, make a rough map of the playground area. Spread 50 cents worth of pennies within about a 20' by 20' area. "Bury" the coins by stepping on them or scuffling the dirt. Go out first thing in the morning to have students begin searching for the pennies. As students find a treasure, they record its location on the map. (Another option is to hide pennies in the classroom and follow these same steps.)

Inventors

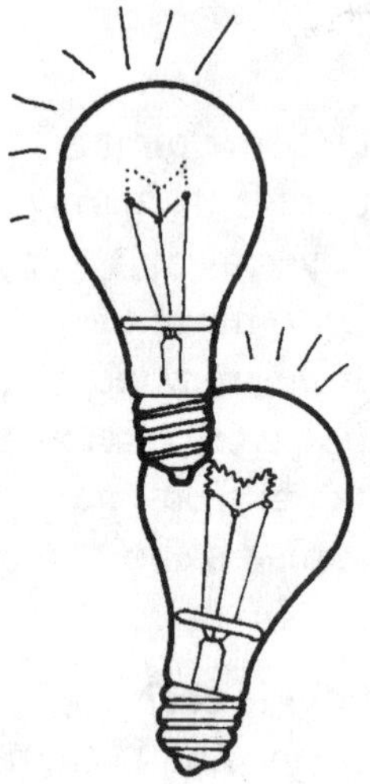

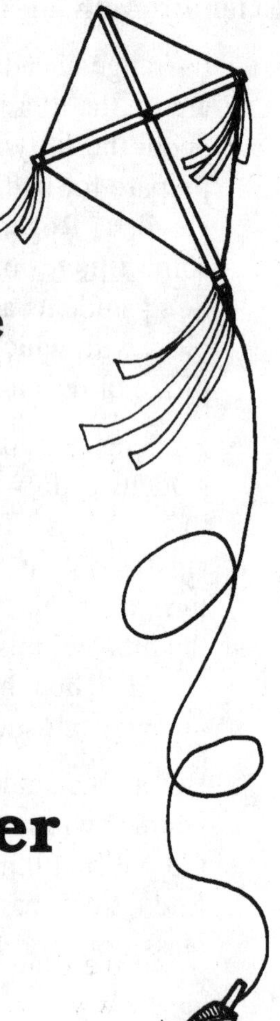

Necessity may be the mother of invention, but for these dedicated individuals, inventing was a way of life. Students learn more about the lives and creations of these imaginative men.

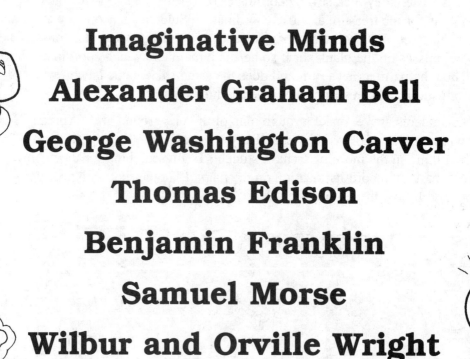

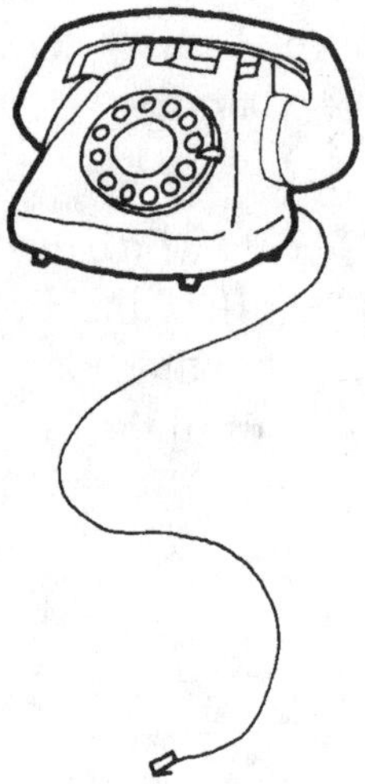

Imaginative Minds

Alexander Graham Bell

George Washington Carver

Thomas Edison

Benjamin Franklin

Samuel Morse

Wilbur and Orville Wright

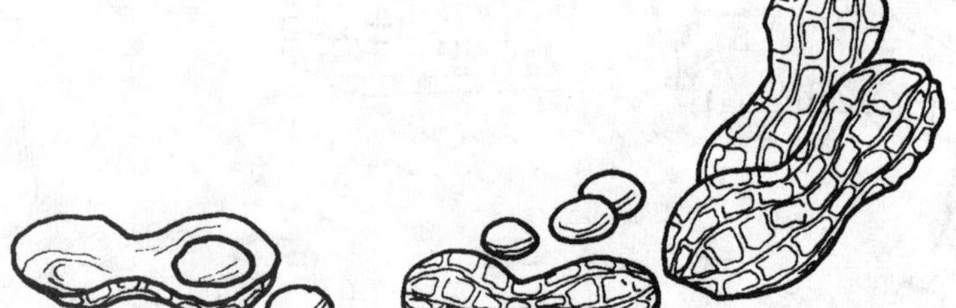

IMAGINATIVE MINDS

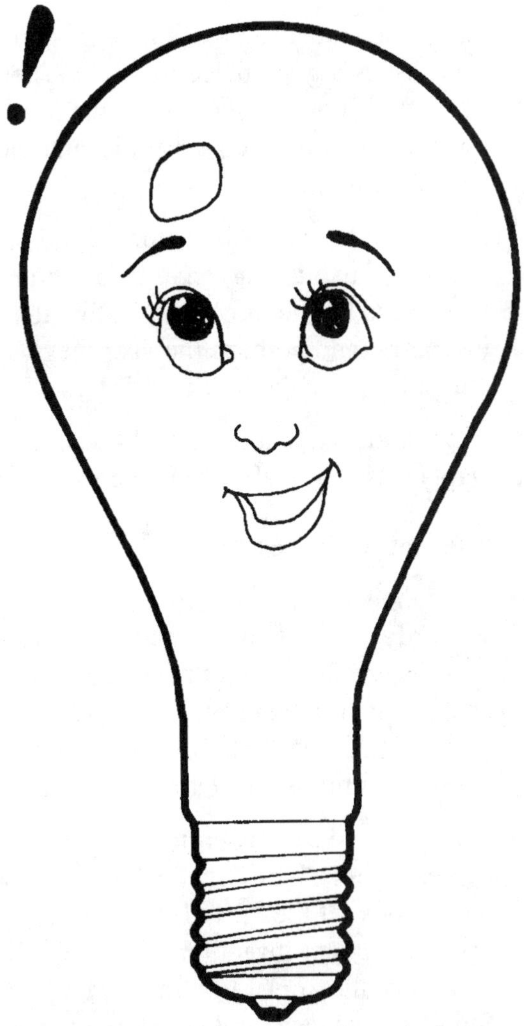

Objective:

The pre-and post-Internet activities that follow complement the inventor activities from pages 20 to 40. Students use what they learned about inventors past and present to create unique and relevant inventions of their own which they display at a class "Invention Convention."

Materials Needed:

- one large cardboard box
- miscellaneous craft supplies
- note cards
- one copy of page 19 per team of students
- handy "junk" (bathroom tissue tubes, foil, cans, yarn, two-liter containers, shoeboxes, craft sticks, cotton, colored plastic wrap, etc.)

Web Sites—Destination URLs:

U.S. Patent Process
http://www.patentspending.com/

Invention Dimension
http://web.mit.edu/invent/

Inventure Place (National Inventors Hall of Fame)
http://www.invent.org/

Build It Yourself
http://northshore.shore.net/~biy/

An Exhibition of the National Museum of American History
Information Age: People, Information & Technology
(Sponsored by the Smithsonian Institution)
http://photo2.si.edu/infoage.html

IMAGINATIVE MINDS *(cont.)*

Pre-Internet Activities:

- Teach the students about the process of applying for a patent. (The site entitled "U.S. Patent Process" is a good place to start.) Then allow teams of students to use their Internet research skills to discover some inventions people have created and patented. Discuss the motivation these inventors had for their creations and the math and science skills that were necessary before they began creating.
- Before investigating inventors of the past, have a small group of students create an "invention machine," using a large cardboard box and miscellaneous craft supplies. While learning about inventions by the famous inventors that follow, write the names of the inventions and their inventors (and perhaps the year they were created) on note cards. Place them in the "invention machine." See the first post-Internet activity below to find out what to do next.
- Have students visit the sites "Invention Dimension" and "Inventure Place" to gather information for a class report about an inventor not mentioned in the following pages.

Post-Internet Activities:

- After the students have completed the activities for all the inventors, students play "Invention Jeopardy." Divide the class into teams. Each team decides on one spokesperson who will stand when he or she knows the correct answer. Assign one person to be the host. He or she selects a card at random and says the name of the invention. The team whose spokesperson stands first gets the first chance to tell who the inventor was to score a point for his or her team. Play continues until all the cards have been "played."
- Host a class-size "Invention Convention" for imaginative minds waiting for an opportunity to express themselves. Students may work in small groups for this activity. For introductory ideas, they may visit the "Build It Yourself" site and click the Famous Inventors link to read about original student inventions on the World Wide Web. When they are ready to begin their own creations, they must first think of an idea for a novel invention and design a model of it on paper. Students may use the Invention guide page 19, to help organize their thoughts. Then they use miscellaneous "junk" to create a working model of their invention. (Like all inventors of the past, if their model doesn't work when they test it, send them "back to the drawing board"!) Once the students have a working model, issue them an imaginary patent number. Then they create a poster explaining the invention's name, use, and a description of how it works to advertise it at the convention. If desired, have the students write a business letter to a prospective development company explaining why they should consider mass producing this idea. When all the students are ready, have an Invention Convention. Post students, creations, and posters around the room or media center. Invite parents and students from other classes to visit the convention to observe and ask questions of the inventors.

FROM THE IMAGINATION OF

Name:____

Directions: Think of an original invention. Consider its purpose and how it works. Write in complete sentences. Draw a diagram of it in the space below. Submit this form and a working model of your invention to your teacher who will issue you a patent number.

The name of my (our) invention is____

It is necessary because ____

____

____

____

The way it works is____

____

____

____

(For Official Use Only) Patent Number: ________________________________

ALEXANDER GRAHAM BELL

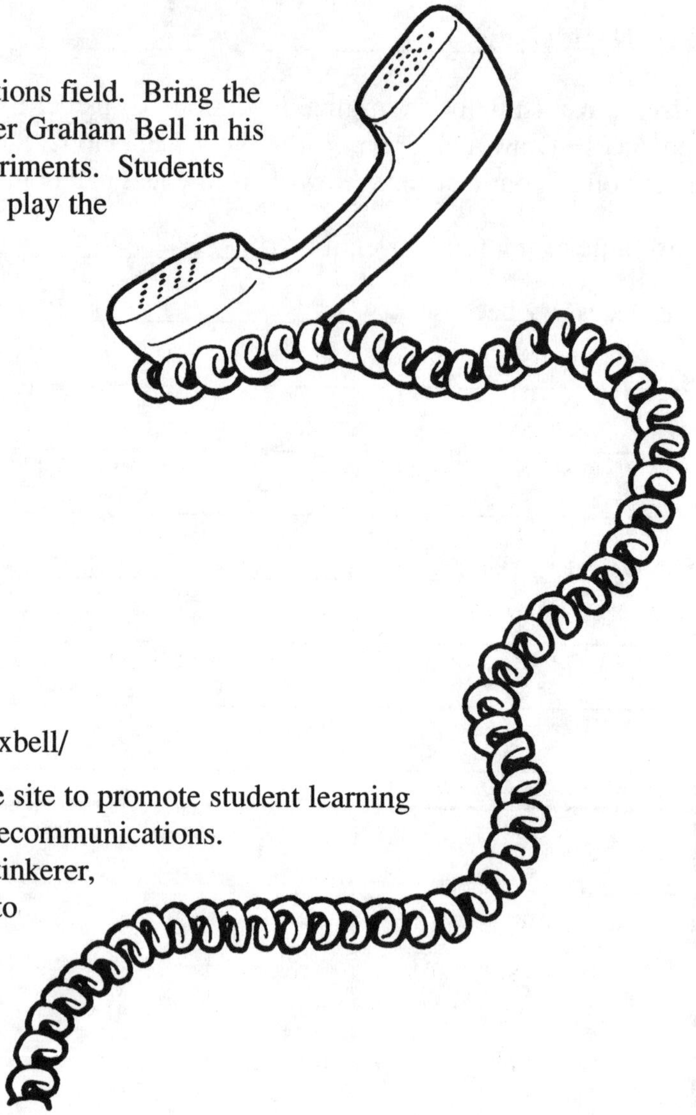

Objective:

Technology is quickly changing the communications field. Bring the students back to when it all began with Alexander Graham Bell in his laboratories conducting innumerable sound experiments. Students learn the "inner" workings of the human ear and play the role of Bell himself by conducting simple sound experiments.

Materials Needed:

- model of the human ear
- wire coat hangers
- string
- one copy of page 22 for each student
- writing paper

Focus Web Site—Destination URLs:

who was? Alexander Graham Bell
http://www.att.com:80/attlabs/brainspin/alexbell/

About This Site: AT&T sponsors this interactive site to promote student learning about the inventor who led the world towards telecommunications. Follow the links to learn about Bell the teacher, tinkerer, and inventor. Along the way, students may link to learn more about the way things work. At the end of the tour of Bell's life, accept the challenge of an "interactivity" or online quiz. The site returns with the students' scores and explanations of missed items.

Alternative Web Sites:

Bell's Telephone
http://sln.fi.edu/franklin/inventor/bell.html

More About Bell
http://www.pbs.org:80/wgbh/pages/amex/technology/telephone/mabell.html

Alexander Graham Bell: The Inventor
http://www.invent.org/book/book-text/7.html

ALEXANDER GRAHAM BELL *(cont.)*

Pre-Internet Activity:

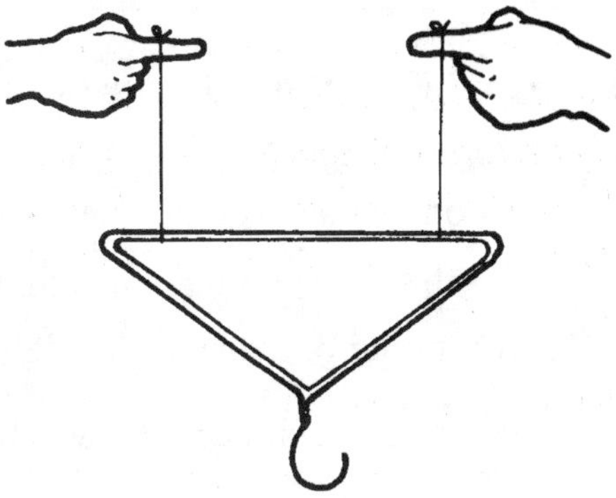

Display a model of the human ear. Discuss how sound travels (sound waves). Conduct this simple sound experiment to show that sound travels differently through various media. Attach yard-long lengths of string to the bottom corners of a wire coat hanger. Wrap the string around each index finger so the hanger is inverted. Tap the length of the hanger with a pencil. Have the students describe the sound. Then ask individual students to wrap the string around their index fingers and place them, gently, in their ears. Tap the hanger once again. Have the students who conduct the demonstration describe the sound to their classmates. Allow an opportunity for all students to experience the new sound. Tell the class that Alexander Graham Bell, whom we know as the inventor of the telephone, was fascinated with sound and vibrations and that they will have a chance to learn more about him on the Internet.

Teaching the Lesson:

1. Distribute a copy of page 22 to each student. Launch the destination URL with the class. Read the introductory paragraphs, and then allow teams of three to five students to follow the links to complete the activity page.
2. Review a model of the human ear. Have students volunteer to explain to the class how our ears change vibrations to intelligible sounds.
3. Have the students pretend they are Alexander Graham Bell conducting valuable sound experiments as part of their research. Have them write a summary of their observations.
   - Make a "telephone" with Styrofoam cups and yarn. Listen to each other across varying distances, trying to communicate with both a taut and sagging "phone line."
   - Calculate the approximate time the sound of a bouncing ball takes to travel across different lengths of the playground.
   - Fill glasses or jars with varying amounts of water. Clink the glasses to produce different pitches of sound.
   - Have the students listen to sound through air by sitting upright and tapping desks with pencils, through water by tapping containers of water while putting their ears to the sides of the containers, and through solids by tapping their desks with pencils while their ears are resting on their desks.
   - Supply varying widths of rubber bands. Have the students pull them to varying degrees of tautness and "twang" them.
   - Have the students record everyday sounds with a tape recorder. They play their recordings for their classmates and have them guess what the sounds are.

ALEXANDER GRAHAM BELL

Name ____

Launch this Web site: http://www.att.com:80/attlabs/brainspin/alexbell/

Directions: Follow the links to learn about Bell as a teacher, tinkerer, and inventor. Read the information and answer the questions.

Click the link to begin reading about Bell, the **Teacher**.

1. What kind of students did Bell teach? ______________________________
2. Where did Bell begin his teaching career? ______________________________
3. What did Bell have to do in order to help deaf people speak? ______________________________

   ____

Click **how does the ear hear?** Read about how the ear works. Number the order in which these events occur each time you hear a sound. Click the <**Back**> arrow from the task bar when you're finished.

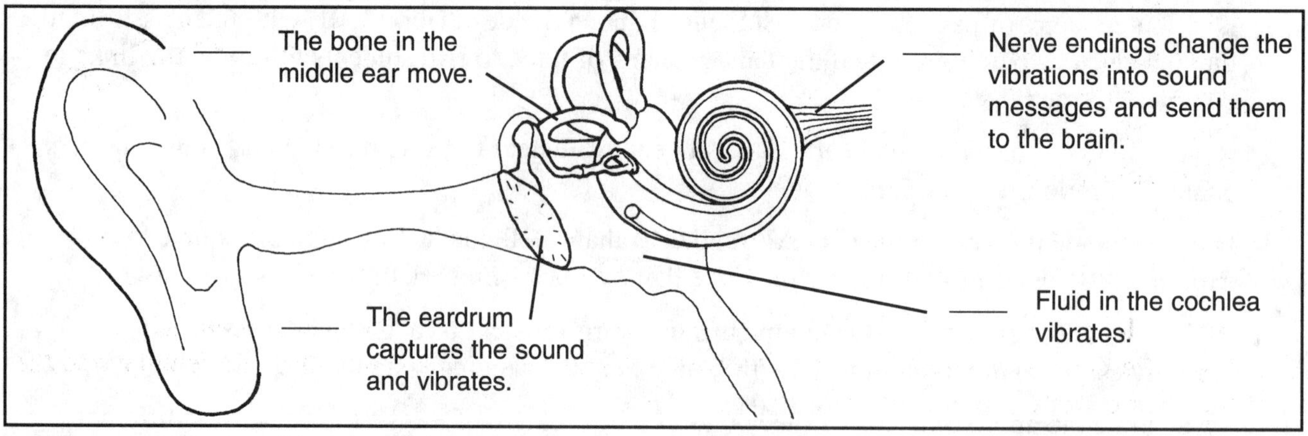

___ The bone in the middle ear move.
___ Nerve endings change the vibrations into sound messages and send them to the brain.
___ The eardrum captures the sound and vibrates.
___ Fluid in the cochlea vibrates.

Click the link to read about Bell, the **Tinkerer**.

4. What invention helped him see sound? ______________________________
5. What did Bell try to teach his dog how to do? ______________________________

Click the link to read about Bell, the **Inventor**.

6. What was Bell's next invention? ______________________________
7. On what date was the **first intelligible sentence** carried over the telephone?

   ______________________________ Click the link to find out what it was.

   Write the words Bell spoke to Watson. ______________________________

   ____

ALEXANDER GRAHAM BELL *(cont.)*

Extended Activities:

- Use the study of Bell as an excuse to have the students practice their telephone manners. Review the words Bell first spoke to Watson over the phone ("Mr. Watson, come here, I want you!"). Discuss how Bell could have been more polite to his science partner. Have the students work in pairs to list three important tips for demonstrating good phone manners. Combine the students' thoughts onto one poster. Then discuss what to say if they are home alone, someone calls whom they don't know, they receive a "silent" caller, etc. Have the students practice phone manners with donated phones from home.
- Students can see an actual sound wave with this simple experiment. Attach a straight pin to the end of a tuning fork so the pin is extended off the end. After twanging the tuning fork, run the pin along a length of wax paper. The sound waves appear on the paper, similar to the way Bell's phonoautograph recorded sound with straw etching sound waves in glass.

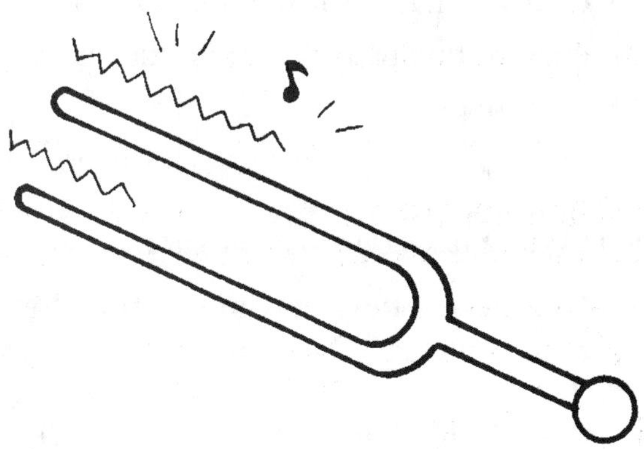

- Students may enjoy these interactive online games. Have students visit the site below and then click on the link **<u>Check Out These Games>>>Grade 3–4 and 5–6</u>**.

  Alexander Graham Bell's Kids Page
  http://bell.uccb.ns.ca:80/kids/kidsindex.htm

- Invite a local telephone worker to discuss with students how phone companies manage the extensive amount of phone line, how communications have changed over the past century, and the future of communications students have to look forward to.

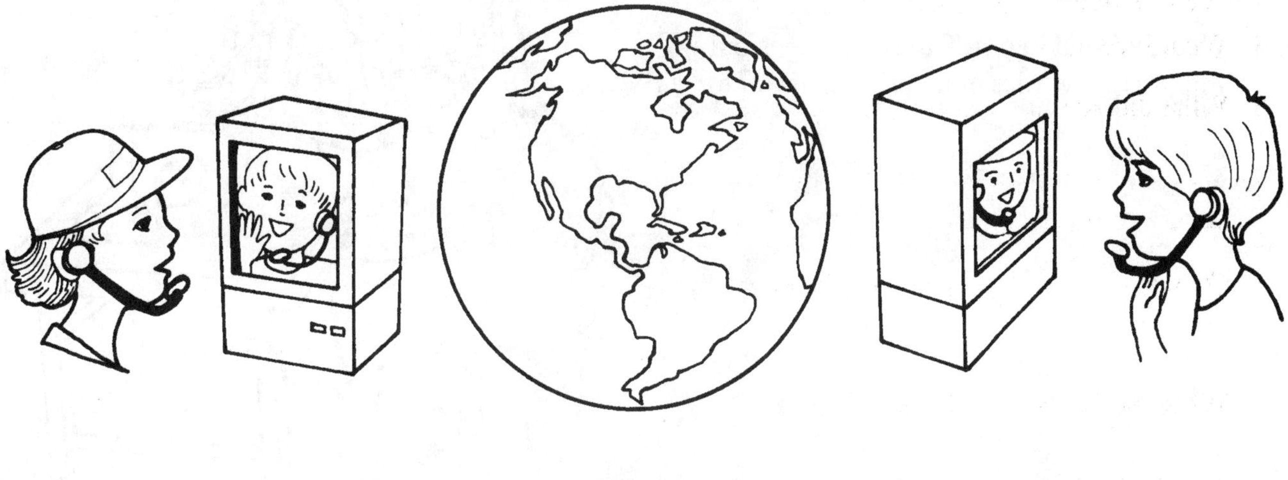

GEORGE WASHINGTON CARVER

Objective:

Inventions are not just contraptions that move and make noise. Students learn that many important discoveries were made by scientists such as George Washington Carver who worked with natural products to create useful synthetic products that are part of their everyday lives. They also decide what they consider his most important accomplishment and defend their views in a class debate.

Materials Needed:

- chalkboard
- empty containers listing the ingredients of bleach, mayonnaise, shampoo, and shaving cream
- construction paper for each student
- magazines
- one copy of page 26 for each student

Focus Web Site—Destination URLs:

George Washington Carver, Jr.: Chemurgist
http://www.lib.lsu.edu/lib/chem/display/carver.html

About This Site: George Washington Carver dedicated his life to creating useful substances made from natural products. At this site are a brief biography and listing of some synthetic products George Washington Carver developed.

Alternative Web Sites:

George Washington Carver National Monument
http://www.coax.net/people/LWF/carver.htm

George Washington Carver
http://www.invent.org/book/book-text/23.html

George Washington Carver (images only)
http://cag-www.lcs.mit.edu/~anne/inventors/GWC/

GEORGE WASHINGTON CARVER *(cont.)*

Pre-Internet Activity:

List these products on the chalkboard: bleach, mayonnaise, shampoo, shaving cream. Bring in an empty container of each common product. Distribute the containers to four students and have them read the ingredients in each product. List them under their headings on the board. Discuss how the students think these products were "invented." Explain that an African American named George Washington Carver was responsible for their production in the late 1800's to early 1900's and that more information about this inventor is awaiting them on the Internet.

Teaching the Lesson:

1. Discuss the difference between natural (from the earth) and synthetic (artificial or man-made) products. Explain that all of the items from the pre-Internet activity are synthetic since they aren't naturally occurring. Have the students cut out pictures from magazines to illustrate each topic; they glue natural products on the front and synthetic products on the back of a sheet of construction paper.
2. Distribute a copy of page 26 to each student. If desired, launch the Web site as a class to complete question number one. Then allow the students to work in small groups to finish reading the information and answering the questions.
3. Review the products from the pre-Internet activity. How do they think these products have changed over the past 100 years or so?
4. Compile a class list of what the students consider to be Mr. Carver's most important discoveries. Have them defend their decisions in a class debate. Students form groups with classmates who agree with their own opinions as to Carver's single most important discovery. Then spokespersons from each group debate with one another in an attempt to persuade their classmates to agree with them.

Extended Activity:

- George Washington Carver is most remembered for his "invention" of peanut butter. Have students "discover" their own synthetic product from this natural one. Students may work in teams of three or four for this activity. Distribute a few peanuts (in the shell) to each group for them to take apart and observe. Then they invent a synthetic product (edible or not) from them. They design a poster of their invention, giving it an original name and explaining its purpose. Then they create an advertisement for their product. When their projects are complete, have the groups share their commercials. Display their posters in the hall under the heading "Peanuts, Peanut Butter, and ?"

GEORGE WASHINGTON CARVER

Name ____

Launch this Web site: http://www.lib.lsu.edu/lib/chem/display/carver.html

Directions: Read the information about George Washington Carver. Answer the questions.

1. What three years are listed as Mr. Carver's birth date? ______________________

   Why do you think there are three years listed? ______________________

   ____

2. Mr. Carver was a former slave. How many professional positions did he hold during his lifetime? ____________ List three. ______________________

   ____

3. What is the definition of chemurgy? ______________________

   ____

4. List three natural products with which Mr. Carver researched the most. Circle the one he developed into the most synthetic products. ______________________

   ____

5. List two industrial products he developed. ______________________

   ____

6. Mr. Carver was the first African American admitted to Simpson College in Iowa. What might have happened if the university had decided to deny his application? ______________________

   ____

   ____

7. Look at the list of products developed by Mr. Carver. Decide on the three most important discoveries. List them here. ______________________

   ____

THOMAS EDISON

Objective:

Why would a near-deaf man invent a sound machine? Why not? These Internet activities reveal a personal look at Thomas Edison's life and his insatiable quest for the "new and improved" machine. Students categorize his inventions and consider the challenges he faced.

Materials Needed:

- note cards
- one copy of page 29 for each student
- writing paper

Focus Web Site—Destination URLs:

Edison Internet Museum
http://www.naples.net/~arzone/edison2.htm

About This Site: Listed here are ten links to grab students' attention about this inventor responsible for the phonograph, electric light, and motion picture as well as many other inventions. Bountiful graphics and good organization of links make this a "student-friendly" site.

Alternative Web Sites:

Thomas Edison Biography
http://edison-ford-estate.com/ed_bio.htm

Thomas Alva Edison
http://www.minot.com/~mps/edison/edison.html

Edison National Historic Site
http://www.nps.gov/edis/ed872000.htm

THOMAS EDISON *(cont.)*

Pre-Internet Activity:

List ten of Edison's inventions (see below—list is just a sample) on note cards. Have the students read the list and choose the ones they think were not inventions of Thomas Edison. Have the students give reasons for their answers. Following a class discussion, tell the students that Edison was responsible for all of the inventions on the cards. Explain that they will have a chance to visit an Internet site to learn more about Edison's life and to discover a great many more of his inventions.

- stock ticker
- typewriter
- advanced telegraphs
- phonograph
- thermoelectric battery
- perforating pens
- telegraph transmitter
- electric motor
- incandescent electric lamp
- talking motion pictures

Teaching the Lesson:

1. Have the students analyze the list of ten inventions and place them into categories (sound machines, electrical machines, etc.). Have them consider each apparatus and conclude which fields of study Edison seemed most interested in (communications, electricity, etc.).

2. Distribute the cards to ten students. Launch the Web site with the class. Link to **Edison Inventions & .wav file**. Have a student volunteer read the introductory paragraph and then the list of inventions. The students with the cards write down the year the invention was created. As a class, list them in the order in which they occurred. (The talking motion picture is dated 1913.)

3. Distribute a copy of page 29 to each student. Allow groups of three to five students turns at the computer to complete the activity page.

4. Have the students review the false statements and rewrite them to make them true on the backside of the page or on a separate sheet of paper.

5. As another mathematical challenge, ask the students to calculate the average number of patents Edison applied for each year of his life. ($1093 \div 84$ = about 13; that's over one for each month of his life—astounding!)

6. Not mentioned in great detail is Edison's hearing loss. Have the students review the list of inventions that involved sound. Then they brainstorm ways Edison could have overcome his handicap to still achieve successful results. Edison's is a remarkable, inspiring, and true story about overcoming adversity. Have the students consider some challenges they have had to overcome. They can each write an essay describing their situation and the results of their efforts.

FACTS ABOUT THOMAS ALVA EDISON

Name ____

Launch this Web site: http://www.naples.net/~arzone/edison2.htm

Directions: Click on the link Edison Biography. Color in the light bulbs beside each true statement about Thomas Edison.

1. Thomas was the oldest of seven children.

2. His middle name is "Alva" in honor of his mother's favorite restaurant.

3. Thomas Edison was not a very bright student.

4. Thomas was homeschooled beginning at the age of ten.

5. Thomas set up a laboratory in the basement.

6. Thomas' first job was as a grocery delivery boy.

7. Thomas learned how to use the telegraph while working for a railway.

8. Thomas destroyed every telegraph he touched.

9. His work with the telegraph led to electrical inventions and the founding of the Edison Electric Company.

10. Soon Edison was powering entire cities with a central power system.

11. Some of Edison's inventions were created simply by accident.

12. The first color motion picture was hand painted.

13. Edison patented more than 5,000 inventions.

Bonus! How old was Edison when he died? ____

THOMAS EDISON *(cont.)*

Extended Activities:

- The phonograph both recorded and played back sound. Edison's first recording was a recitation of the nursery rhyme, "Mary Had a Little Lamb." Recording devices have come a long way since then. Have the students take advantage of the efficiency of modern recording devices by recording themselves reading a short story on a tape recorder. Then they bring their book and the cassette to a reading buddy in a lower grade and play the recording to share the book.
- Remarkable words about remarkable inventions will be all the students can think about with this alliteration activity. Assign small groups of students to fill in words to fit each category with words that have the same beginning sound as one of Edison's inventions. Assign as many parts of speech categories as the students need to practice. Then they use words from their lists to create original alliterative sentences.

Invention	Adjectives	Proper Nouns	Verbs
phonograph	funny	Phil	fix
	philosophical	Florida	fight
	physical	Philippines	fly/flew

- Philosophical Phil flew to the Philippines with a physical phonograph.
- Lovely Lily laughed at the lively light bulb in Lexington.

Have the students make banners of their sentences by either writing them on sentence strips or typing them as banners in a desktop publishing program.

- Edison was responsible for engineering the first central powered city. How would our lives be different without electricity? Challenge the class to keep a log of every electrical appliance they use throughout the day. When they return to school the next day, discuss any difficulties the students might have living without those devices. In fact, many students who have lived through powerful storms may have already had this experience. Allow them time to share their stories. Then have the students write a creative story describing a day when the electricity went out.

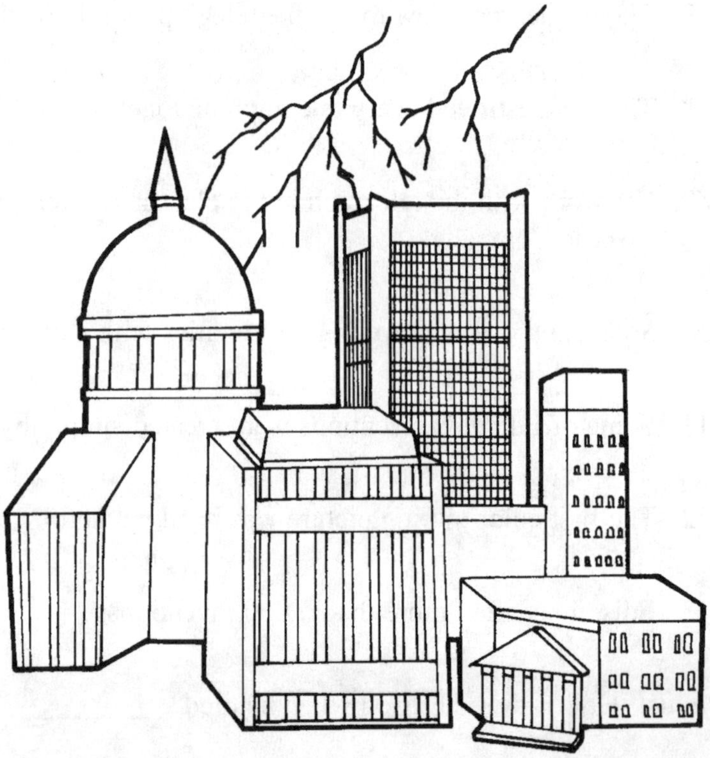

BENJAMIN FRANKLIN

Objective:

Students may know Benjamin Franklin as an important political figure of the 18th century—or perhaps as an inventor responsible for the creation of the Franklin stove. Or as a scientist who toyed with lightning and electricity. Students will learn that Benjamin Franklin was all these and more when they link to Web pages with information about seven professional roles to which he aspired. Then they apply their creative thinking skills to design and create hats for Benjamin Franklin to wear while taking on those roles.

Materials Needed:

- chalkboard
- 4–6 copies of page 33
- miscellaneous art supplies
- note cards

Focus Web Site—Destination URLs:

Benjamin Franklin: Glimpses of the Man
http://sln.fi.edu/franklin/rotten.html

About This Site: Each of Benjamin Franklin's seven professions links to information about that area of his life. Students get a "glimpse" of the real man at every turn, beginning with a memorable quote and downloadable *Quicktime* movie.

Alternative Web Sites:

The Autobiography of Benjamin Franklin
http://earlyamerica.com/lives/franklin/index.html

Ben Franklin: A Documentary History
http://www.english.udel.edu/lemay/franklin

BENJAMIN FRANKLIN *(cont.)*

Pre-Internet Activity:

List on the chalkboard the following professions Franklin held during his life: scientist, inventor, statesman, printer, philosopher, musician, and economist. Have the students give a brief definition of each term and tell what a person with this profession would do. Then tell them that Benjamin Franklin was all these things and more and that they will have a chance to learn more about these areas of his life on the Internet.

Teaching the Lesson:

1. Divide the class into four to six groups. Write one of the link titles (all the professions listed in the pre-Internet activity except "philosopher") at the top of each activity sheet on page 33. Give each group an activity sheet with a different link title. Each group is responsible for gathering information for the topic listed at the top of their page. (The "musician" and "economist" links are rather brief. Students accessing these links may have difficulty completing the activity page. The "philosopher" link has virtually no information at all.)

2. Launch the Web site as a class. Read the quote at the top. Have the students tell what Franklin's message is in their own words. Read the introductory paragraphs, and then allow the group with the first link, **scientist**, to work independently.

3. Allow each subsequent group in the links about Ben Franklin's life their turn to complete page 33.

4. After all the groups have finished researching, have them summarize their information in a class report. They use their designs to create hats related to those professions in Franklin's life. Then they don their chapeaus and share their reports with the class.

5. Display the students' hats in the hall with brief explanations as to their significance (written on note cards) on a bulletin board entitled "The Many Hats of Benjamin Franklin."

Benjamin Franklin was a philosopher. He thought a lot about his vision for the future of the United States.

BENJAMIN FRANKLIN, ____________

Name ____

Launch this Web site: http://sln.fi.edu/franklin/rotten.html

Directions: Click on the link above. Read the information and fill in the blanks. Use additional paper, if necessary.

Write a brief definition of the term. ____

____

Tell what Ben Franklin did to be considered one of these professionals. ______________________

____

List a few examples of his work. ____

____

____

____

Write some other interesting facts you learned here. ____

____

____

____

Click on one of the links on this Web page. Write a short summary telling what you learned.

____

____

____

____

____

Think about the kind of hat Franklin may have worn while he acted as this professional. Draw it on the backside of this paper.

BENJAMIN FRANKLIN *(cont.)*

Extended Activity:

Benjamin Franklin was not just responsible for the inventions of things; he had a natural talent for creating useful phrases with words as well. Introduce the students to *Poor Richard's Almanack.* Have the students work with a partner to access the **printer** link from the focus Web site, and then click on **What do you think Ben meant?** at the bottom of the page. The students will see an alphabetical listing of some of Poor Richard's proverbs. They select one they find most appealing, write it down, then reword the ending to create a new proverb. The partners work in word processing to make two headlines: "Poor Richard says... (followed by Poor Richard's proverb)" and "Poor (their names) say...(followed by their revised proverb)." The students print their work and then illustrate the meaning of the proverb. Combine them into one book entitled "Poor (teacher's name) Almanack."

Students may also glimpse some of Poor Richard's sayings by accessing the following Web site, then clicking the link **Ben Franklin, Energy Saver?**

Poor Richard's Energy Almanac
http:www.energy.ca.gov/energy/education/ben/ben-html/benfranklin.html

Poor Richard says . . .

He that lieth down with dogs, shall rise up with fleas.

Poor Jim and Kyle say . . .

He that lies down with dogs, shall find mud in his fur.

SAMUEL MORSE

Objective:

With all the work being done to extend communications long distances, we have Samuel Morse to thank for its initial success. Students learn the necessity of his invention, Morse code, and how it helped launch society into the communications age. Then they try their own hand at coding and decoding a message using Morse code.

Materials Needed:

- pencil with an eraser
- one copy of page 37 for each student
- printed copy of Morse code (optional—from the focus Web site, link to **The Codes**)

Focus Web Site—Destination URLs:

Telegraph Lore
http://www.cris.com/~Gsraven/index.shtml

About This Site: Students may not be into collecting telegraph keys yet, but they may find an interest after visiting this site about the complete history of the telegraph. From history to folklore to mechanics, the information at this site will satisfy the most curious of telegraph enthusiasts.

Alternative Web Sites:

Canadian Railway Telegraph History Web Site
http://web.idirect.com/~rburnet/

Morsum Magnificat
http://www.morsum.demon.co.uk/

Morse Biography: "What Hath God Brought"
http://www.acusd.edu/~ekarakis/Morse.html

SAMUEL MORSE *(cont.)*

Pre-Internet Activity:

Assign each student a partner. Challenge them to tap messages to their partners with the eraser ends of their pencils. Both partners should have a turn. After about five minutes of tapping, discuss whether this was an easy or difficult task and why. Ask the students what they could do to help make their tapping messages easier to understand. Explain that Samuel Morse is famous for his invention of a universal tapping code used over telegraph lines that enabled anyone to understand the message. They will learn more about him on the Internet.

Teaching the Lesson:

1. Explain that in the early days of long distance communication, people used a telegraph line. Samuel Morse was responsible for creating a simple code which enabled everyone who used the telegraph to easily comprehend the message—after a great deal of practice!

2. Distribute a copy of page 37 to each student. Allow students to work independently or in small groups to launch the Web site, select the appropriate link, and answer the questions.

3. After everyone has completed the activity page, allow students to access the **The Codes** link and write a simple message in Morse code. Students then trade papers and revisit the site and link to decipher their classmates' messages. (Another option is to print **The Codes** Web page and make it available for all students.)

4. Have students use a listing of the Morse code symbols to try tapping another message with their partner, as they did during the pre-Internet activity. Discuss the amount of training necessary to become proficient in the use of Morse code. The following Web sites offer information about learning Morse code and the code itself.

    Morse Code and the Phonetic Alphabet
    http://www.soton.ac.uk/~scp93ch/refer/alphabet.html

    What is the best way to learn Morse Code?
    http://www.acs.ncsu.edu/HamRadio/FAQ/Part_3.2.html

Extended Activities:

- With a copy of the code handy, have the students practice tapping out their spelling words in Morse code.

- Link to **Telegraph Tales** from the focus Web site during oral reading time.

THE MORSE INVENTION

Name ____

Launch this Web site: http://www.cris.com/~Gsraven/index.html

Directions: Link to **A Brief History of the Morse Telegraph**. Read the information and answer the questions.

1. Who invented Morse code? When? ____

   ____

2. What takes the place of letters and numbers? ____

3. Draw a picture on the backside of this page illustrating the sequence of events that take place when using Morse code over a telegraph line. Label these items on your picture: operator, tapping, electrical signals, telegraph line, receiving operator.

4. Who was thought to be Morse's partner in the development of the code? ______________________

   ____

5. What kind of cables distorted the spaced dots? ____

6. What new code was invented to solve this problem? ____

7. List four places or companies where Morse code and the telegraph were used.

   ______________________ ______________________

   ______________________ ______________________

8. What eventually replaced the Morse operator? ____

9. True or false? Morse code is still practiced today. ____

WILBUR AND ORVILLE WRIGHT

Objective:

The Wright brothers are credited with producing and successfully flying the world's first "heavier-than-air" flying machine. Students learn the history of these two famous brothers and then demonstrate the physical factors Wilbur thought had ensured their success.

Materials Needed:

- writing paper
- drawing paper
- one copy of page 40 for each student
- nine-by-twelve-inch construction paper

Focus Web Site—Destination URLs:

The Wright Brothers
http://www.hfmgv.org/histories/wright/wrights.html

About This Site: Students follow the Wright brothers from their humble beginnings in Millville, Indiana, and Dayton, Ohio, to their remarkable flight of the first motor-driven aircraft. When the world said it couldn't be done, Wilbur and Orville astounded the world with their invention achieved by persistence and stick-to-it-iveness.

Alternative Web Sites:

Wilbur Wright—American Inventor
http://www2.lucidcafe.com/lucidcafe/library/96apr/wrightw.html

Orville Wright—American Inventor
http://www2.lucidcafe.com/lucidcafe/library/95aug/wright.html

Wright 1903 Flyer: First Successful Flight (sponsored by the Smithsonian Institution)
http://www.nasm.edu/GALLERIES/GAL100/wright1903.html

The Wright Brothers Aeroplane
http://hawaii.cogsci.uiuc.edu/invent/i/Wrights/library/Century.html

WILBUR AND ORVILLE WRIGHT *(cont.)*

Pre-Internet Activity:

Instruct students to fold a sheet of paper twice to make three columns. Have them consider all the animals that can naturally fly. They write their list down the first column. In the second column, they list items that are extremely light and seem to "float" in air or blow easily in the wind (feathers, paper, etc.). In the third column, they list every apparatus they can think of that flies but doesn't use a powered motor (hang glider, paper airplane, kite, etc.) Have them look over the three lists and consider the elements of nature that apply when any of these things take flight. Ask them how considering this might be important when designing an aircraft. Then have them illustrate one item from each list as it flies. Attach their artwork to a bulletin board entitled "Into the Wild Blue Yonder." Explain that the Wright brothers were determined to successfully fly a motor-driven aircraft when the world was saying it couldn't be done. They will learn more about this historic flight on the Internet.

Teaching the Lesson:

1. Distribute a copy of page 40 to each student. Launch the Web site with the class. Point out that they will have to click a link to answer number eight and then click **<back>** again to complete the page. Demonstrate this action if the students are unfamiliar with it.

2. Allow the students time to work independently or in small groups to complete the activity page.

3. Have the students make a simple paper airplane with a nine-by-twelve-inch piece of construction paper. Use this three-dimensional figure to demonstrate the three axes of motion Wilbur considered when designing his aircraft (pitch, roll, and yaw). Explain that because of this consideration, he was really the only aircraft inventor at the time who would meet with success.

4. Have the students fly their paper airplanes. Then they redesign their model to try to make it fly farther and longer.

Extended Activity:

Students who are very interested in learning more about this famous first flight can read the entire account as written by Orville Wright himself by visiting this site:

How We Made First Flight by Orville Wright
http://hawaii.cogsci.uiuc.edu/invent/i/Wrights/library/Century.html

This site offers the viewer a thorough graphic display of the Wright brothers and their involvement with the "flying machine."

The Wright Brothers Photographs
http://hawaii.cogsci.uiuc.edu/invent/i/Wrights/Wright_photos.html

A FAMOUS FIRST FLIGHT

Name ____

Launch this Web site: http://www.hfmgv.org/histories/wright/wrights.html

Directions: Read the information and answer the questions.

1. Who was the older of the two famous Wright brothers? ____________________
2. What gift began the boys' interest in flight? ____________________
3. Write a sentence telling about their education. ____________________

   ____
4. What was their first career as "the Wright brothers"? ____________________
5. What kind of shop did they open in 1893? ____________________
6. Who did Wilbur turn to for help in aeronautical research? ____________________

   ____
7. What were the three elements of flying, according to Wilbur? ____________________

   ____
8. Label the **three axes of motion**.

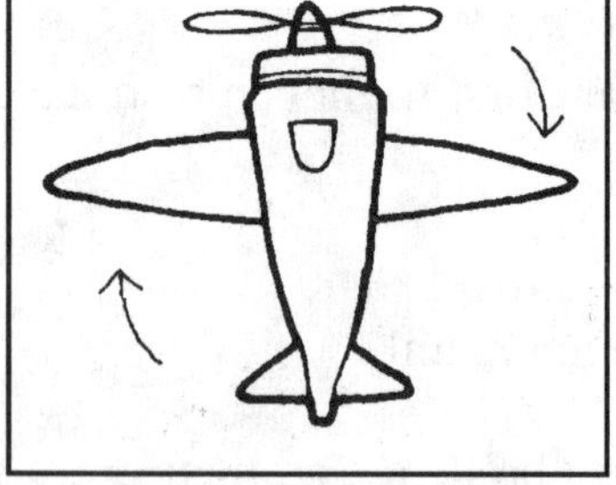

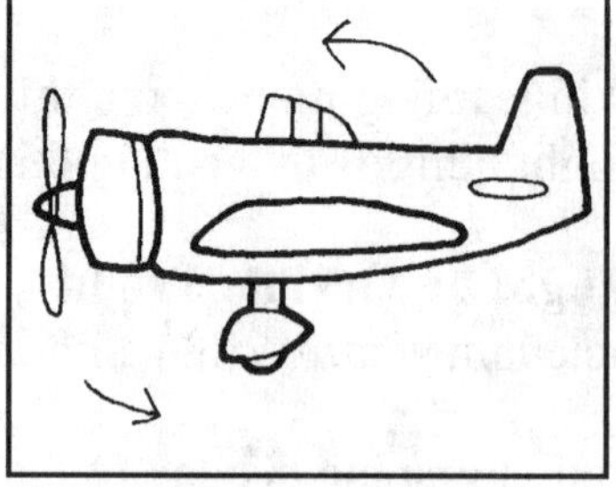

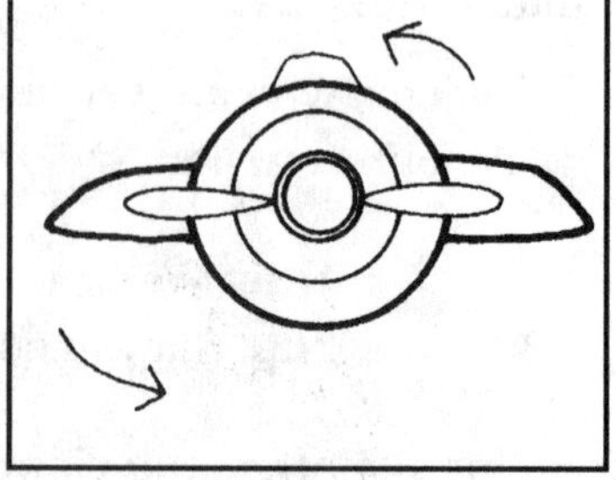

____________________ ____________________ ____________________

9. What kind of equipment did Wilbur use to test his wing theory? ____________________
10. Who made the historic first flight? ____________________

    What was the date? ____________________ How long did it last? ____________________

People in U.S. History

Students will marvel at the accomplishments others have made toward our society by completing Internet activities about these famous people from our nation's past.

The Presidents

Susan B. Anthony

Albert Einstein

Martin Luther King, Jr.

Rosa Parks

Jackie Robinson

THE PRESIDENTS

Objective:

Students will value this chance to research freely on the Internet as they investigate the presidents in U.S. history. They may follow the suggested Internet search instructions or use a search engine of their choosing to find appropriate sites from which to gather information.

Materials Needed:

- chalkboard or chart paper
- scrap paper
- writing paper
- small note cards
- one copy of page 44 for each team of students
- half sheet ($8^1/_2$ by $5^1/_2$ inches) of plain Xerox paper for each team
- colorful construction paper measuring 9 by 6 inches for each team
- large note cards
- drawing paper

Focus Web Site—Destination URLs:

Potus: Presidents of the United States
http://www.ipl.org/ref/POTUS/

About This Site: This user-friendly presidential resource Web site is full of interesting facts and trivia about every president in U.S. history. Students click on the president of their choosing and then select from one of the many category links to learn more about specific areas of the presidents' lives. Included, also, are highlighted Internet links to additional sites and Web pages for those who wish to "dig deeper."

Alternative Web Sites:

The American President
http://www.grolier.com/presidents/preshome.html

Inaugural Addresses of the Presidents of the United States
http://www.columbia.edu/acis/bartleby/inaugural

Miscellaneous Search Engines
(see listing on page 10)

THE PRESIDENTS (cont.)

Pre-Internet Activity:

Have the students brainstorm a list of personality traits they feel must be present in someone seeking the presidency. Write the traits they mention on the chalkboard or on chart paper. After the students feel the list is fairly complete, have them consider whether the current president possesses all of those traits. Discuss both positive and questionable actions the current president has taken which cause the students to assign or deny him the traits listed on the board. Have the students work in teams of three or four to decide on the five most important traits a president must have. They write them down on a small sheet of scrap paper. Gather the class together and tally the results. Circle the five traits with the most votes. The students then consider whether they could be president based on the list of the five most important qualities of a president.

Teaching the Lesson:

1. Allow the students to work in teams of two or three. List each president and his term(s) in office on a small note card. Have the students randomly select a president to research by choosing from the stack of cards.
2. Distribute a copy of page 44 to each team. They search the Internet using the URL and directions on the page or opt to try their luck with a reliable search engine of their choice. Students may use more traditional research materials if their Internet search does not supply them with the answers to all the questions on the research guide.
3. Once their research is complete, students draw a pencil drawing of their president on a half sheet of plain copy paper (8 1/2 by 5 1/2 inches) and then mount it onto a sheet of colorful construction paper measuring 9 by 6 inches. On a plain large note card they write the president's name in bold letters with a colored marker and write underneath his name brief facts they would like to share with a pen.
4. Have the students each consider their president's greatest accomplishment while he was in office. Have them design and create on a sheet of drawing paper a certificate of achievement for their president.
5. Post the students' artwork, fact cards, and certificates in the hall for others to appreciate.
6. (Optional) Have the students use their research guides to write summary reports of their presidents in a word processing program. Combine all the students' pages to make one book entitled "Presidential Publication."

The Presidents and Their Terms in Office

George Washington	1776–1797	James Buchanan	1857–1861	Warren G. Harding	1921–1923
John Adams	1797–1801	Abraham Lincoln	1861–1865	Calvin Coolidge	1923–1929
Thomas Jefferson	1801–1809	Andrew Johnson	1865–1869	Herbert Hoover	1929–1933
James Madison	1809–1817	Ulysses S. Grant	1869–1877	Franklin D. Roosevelt	1933–1945
James Monroe	1817–1825	Rutherford B Hayes	1877–1881	Harry S. Truman	1945–1953
John Q. Adams	1825–1829	James A. Garfield	1881	Dwight D. Eisenhower	1953–1961
Andrew Jackson	1829–1837	Chester A. Arthur	1881–1885	John F. Kennedy	1961–1963
Martin Van Buren	1837–1841	Grover Cleveland	1885–1889	Lyndon B. Johnson	1963–1969
William H. Harrison	1841	Benjamin Harrison	1889–1893	Richard M. Nixon	1969–1974
John Tyler	1841–1845	Grover Cleveland	1893–1897	Gerald R. Ford	1974–1977
James K. Polk	1845–1849	William McKinley	1897–1901	James E. Carter	1977–1981
Zachary Taylor	1849–1850	Theodore Roosevelt	1901–1909	Ronald W. Reagan	1981–1989
Millard Fillmore	1850–1853	William H. Taft	1909–1913	George H. W. Bush	1989–1993
Franklin Pierce	1853–1857	Woodrow Wilson	1913–1921	William J. B. Clinton	1993–

PRESIDENTIAL RESEARCH GUIDE

Name ____

Launch this Web site: http://www.ipl.org/ref/POTUS/

Directions: Click on the president you are researching. Then select related category links to find the information below. Use additional paper when necessary.

1. Our President (full name) ______________________________________
2. Date born to date died ______________________________________
3. Wife's name ______________________________________
4. Children's names ______________________________________
5. Educational background ______________________________________
6. Career before presidency ______________________________________
7. Party ______________________________________
8. Running mate ______________________________________
9. Election opponent(s) ______________________________________
10. Campaign slogan ______________________________________
11. Number of terms in office and dates ______________________________________
12. How he took office ______________________________________
13. Accomplishments while in office ______________________________________

    ____

    ____
14. Personal history ______________________________________

    ____

    ____
15. Other interesting information ______________________________________

    ____

THE PRESIDENTS *(cont.)*

Extended Activities:

- Have the students revisit the Internet Web site from which they gathered their information. They read carefully for little-known facts about their president and then write three simple trivia statements each on small note cards with the name of their president. Play "Presidential Trivia" one day during social studies. Divide the class into teams. Each team designates a spokesperson. Assign one student to read the trivia cards. When the teams think they know the answer, the spokesperson stands up. The reader calls on the first person to stand. If the spokesperson answers correctly, he/she wins one point for the team. If he/she answers incorrectly, the second person to stand has a chance to answer, and so on. Continue play until all the cards have been read. Place the cards at a learning center for students to study during their free time.

  Can students discover the answers to the following presidential trivia questions?

  - Who was the first American-born president? M. Van Buren
  - Which two presidents died on the same day? What was the date? J. Adams & T. Jefferson; July 4, 1826
  - Who was the shortest president? J. Madison (5' 4")
  - Which president held office for the shortest amount of time? W. Harrison (one month)
  - Which president was the first to get married in the White House? G. Cleveland
  - Which president had a pet cow? H. Taft
  - Which President gave the longest inaugural speech? W. Harrison (That's how he caught pneumonia and died so shortly after taking office.)

- Review some current "hot topics" the students are concerned about. Discuss the topic of campaign promises and how people running for the presidency address the issues that concern both themselves and the public the most. As president, the students may have a chance to correct a social wrong they consider needs attention. Have the students write an essay entitled "If I Were President . . ." They identify a current problem or situation they would like to see resolved and then explain possible ways they would go about correcting it if they were president. With parental permission, submit the students' writings to a local newspaper for publication.

- Review some campaign slogans the students discovered as they conducted their presidential research. Have them use what they know about their president to create an original campaign slogan for him. They design and create a campaign poster with their slogan as if that person were running for office today. Post them around the building for others to view. Students may also make campaign buttons if a button-making machine is available for this task. Encourage the students to wear their buttons each day during a unit about the presidents.

SUSAN B. ANTHONY

Objective:

People throughout the nation's history have struggled to achieve equality for all. Susan B. Anthony began her quest for equal voting rights for women in 1872 and worked toward her goal throughout her life. Her story is one of many successful achievements made by people willing to take a stand and fight for what they believed was just. Students experience her motivation firsthand as they learn about her life, her struggle, and her eventual success.

Materials Needed:

- one copy of page 48 for each student
- writing paper

Focus Web Site—Destination URLs:

Susan B. Anthony House Museum and National Landmark
http://www.susanbanthonyhouse.org/

About This Site: Take a tour of the home of Susan B. Anthony (now a museum and national landmark) in Rochester, N.Y. Visit each floor of her house to get a better understanding of how she lived. Other links of interest include a time line and biography.

Alternative Web Sites:

Susan B. Anthony
http://www.history.rochester.edu/class/sba/first.htm

Susan B. Anthony
http://inform.umd.edu/Pictures/WomensStudies/PictureGallery/anthony.html

Susan B. Anthony
http://www.glue.umd.edu/~cliswp/Bios/sbabio.html

Quotes from Susan B. Anthony
http://www.sba-list.org/quotes.htm

SUSAN B. ANTHONY *(cont.)*

Pre-Internet Activity:

Ask the students what they think might happen to them if they were to try to vote in the next election. Take a poll to see how many students would be interested in voting if they had the opportunity. Why can't they vote? Do they think the legal voting age of eighteen is fair? Why do they think eighteen is the age the lawmakers chose? Explain that women and minorities didn't used to have the right to vote. This was a privilege saved only for white, wealthy, male landowners. As times changed, though, Congress passed several amendments to the Constitution addressing the right to vote by all citizens. Susan B. Anthony led the suffrage movement, which eventually resulted in the passing of the nineteenth amendment. This ensured women the right to vote.

Teaching the Lesson:

1. Review the 14th and 15th amendments to the Constitution. The 14th outlawed slavery by guaranteeing citizenship to each person born in the United States. The 15th ensured that all men could vote regardless of race, color, or previous servitude. These two amendments prompted Susan B. Anthony to take action to obtain equal voting rights for women.

2. Distribute a copy of page 48 to each student. Launch the Web site as a class. Point out the first three links the students may access to learn about Susan B. Anthony. Follow the Online Tour link and read the "Welcome" page with the students. Continue to the Next link with the class, or allow students to work in small groups to tour her house and complete the student activity page.

3. The 19th amendment to the Constitution is sometimes referred to as the "Susan B. Anthony Amendment." Have students consider why her name should be associated with this amendment when it passed in 1920, fourteen years after her death. What must have occurred after her death? Why do they think this amendment took so long to pass? Have a small group of students further research the history behind Amendment 19.

4. Ms. Anthony is quoted as saying, "Failure is impossible." Discuss the philosophy behind this motivating phrase. Do the students believe this is true? What ingredients must be present to meet with success? Was Ms. Anthony a failure because she didn't achieve her goal during her lifetime? Have the students write a brief story telling of a time when they believed failure was impossible, including the goal they were trying to achieve and how they worked to succeed.

AT HOME WITH SUSAN B. ANTHONY

Name ____

Launch this Web site: http://www.susanbanthonyhouse.org/

Directions: Link to take an **Online Tour** of the Susan B. Anthony home. Read the "Welcome" page, then link to the **Next** page on the tour. Read the information and then draw a line to match the room with its historic event.

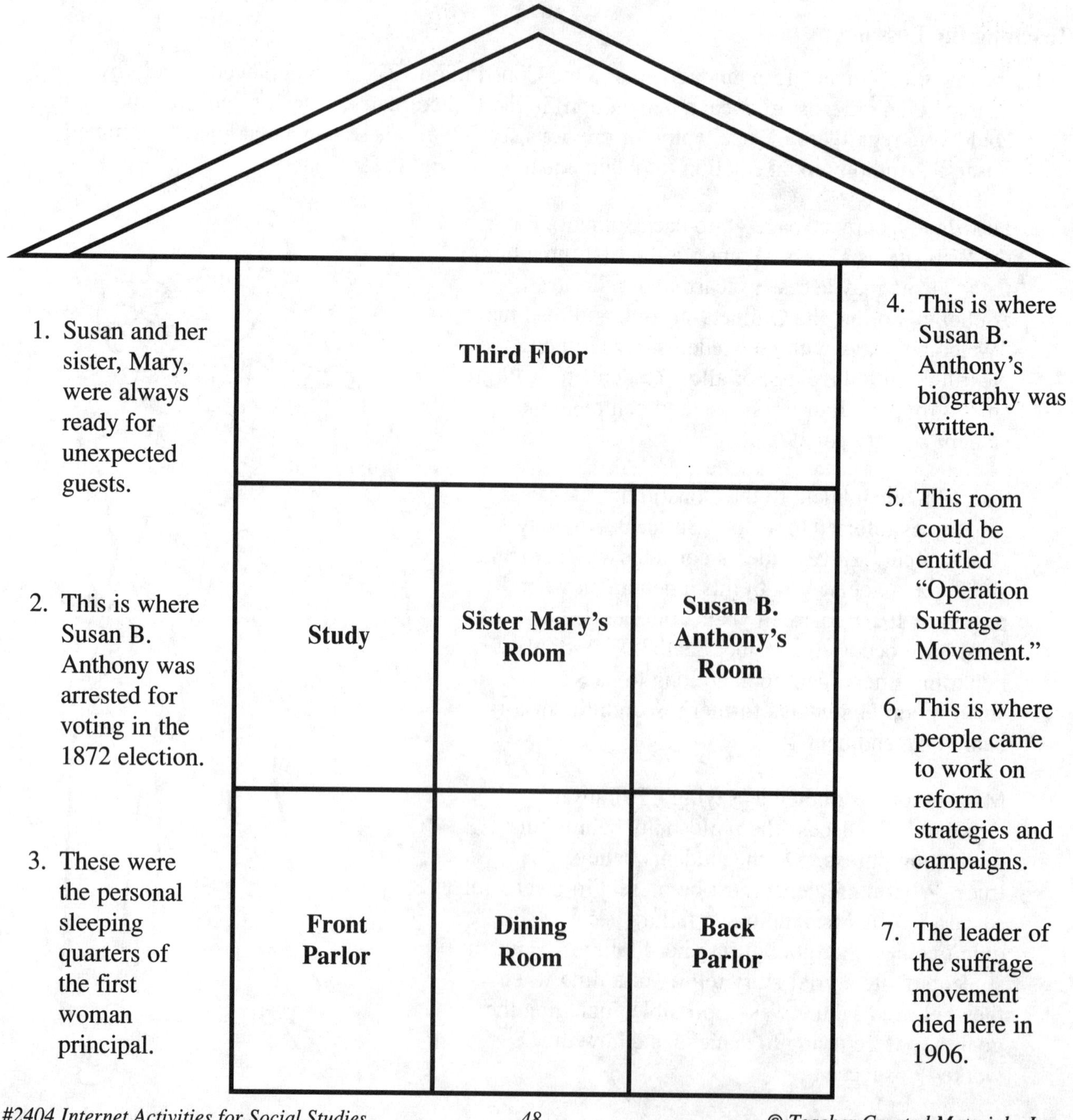

1. Susan and her sister, Mary, were always ready for unexpected guests.
2. This is where Susan B. Anthony was arrested for voting in the 1872 election.
3. These were the personal sleeping quarters of the first woman principal.
4. This is where Susan B. Anthony's biography was written.
5. This room could be entitled "Operation Suffrage Movement."
6. This is where people came to work on reform strategies and campaigns.
7. The leader of the suffrage movement died here in 1906.

ALBERT EINSTEIN

Objective:

Einstein's work proved him to be a true genius, as the name *Einstein* has come to mean. Students learn about important events that occurred in his life and then consider a lighter side to the world's most famous physicist.

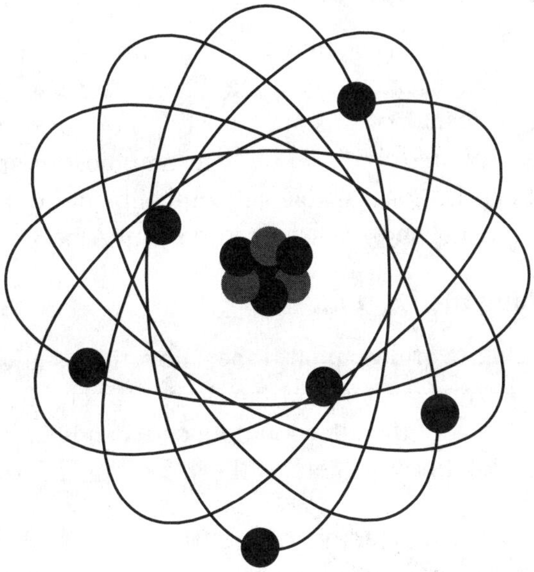

Materials Needed:

- chalkboard
- world map or globe
- one copy of page 51 for each student
- drawing paper for each student

Focus Web Site—Destination URLs:

The Albert Einstein Page
http://www.geocities.com/CapeCanaveral/Lab/3555/

About This Site: Students follow the links to read about five phases of Einstein's life. Brief summaries and accompanying photographs combine to make this an ideal site for young learners. Students can even get a glimpse of Einstein sticking out his tongue for the camera!

Alternative Web Sites:

Einstein Revealed (sponsored by NOVA)
http://www.pbs.org/wgbh/pages/nova/einstein/

Albert Einstein
http://cad.ucla.edu/~andy/einstein.html

Albert Einstein
http://www-groups.dcs.st-and.ac.uk/~history/Mathematicians/Einstein.html

Albert Einstein Online
http://www.westegg.com/einstein/

ALBERT EINSTEIN *(cont.)*

Pre-Internet Activity:

Have the students share what they think is meant when someone is referred to as a "real Einstein." Write his best known formula, $E = mc^2$, on the chalkboard. Have the students share their thoughts as to the significance of this mathematical formula and its relevance to Einstein. Then explain that this was his *special theory of relativity*; as an object approaches the speed of light, time begins to slow down. It is Einstein's most notable accomplishment but by far not his only one. Explain to the students that they will have a chance to learn more about Albert Einstein on the Internet.

Teaching the Lesson:

1. On a world map or globe, show the locations Einstein lived during his lifetime: Ulm, Munich, and Berlin, Germany; Milan, Italy; Zurich, Switzerland; Princeton, New Jersey, U.S.A. Write the names of the cities on note cards and challenge the students to place them in the order in which Einstein lived there as they read this information at the Web site.

2. Distribute a copy of page 51 to each student. Have the students work in small groups to access the Web site, follow the links, and complete the activity page.

3. Einstein may seem like someone who regarded everything as serious business, but students may think otherwise when they get a glimpse of **The Tongue!!!** (a link from the main index). Visit this link as a class. Then have students draw a picture of Einstein doing something they wouldn't ordinarily consider him doing (bowling? Rollerblading? playing video games?). Have them share their work and then post their pictures around the time line bulletin board (see extended activity below).

Extended Activity:

Have the students make a time line of events that occurred in Einstein's life. Divide the class into five teams, one for each link. Assign each group a different link to access: **Childhood**, **Early Career**, **First Breakthrough**, **Second Marriage**, and **Final Years**. Have each group revisit the Web site and select the **To main Index** link and then their assigned link from the list. They write down spotlighted years and the events that took place in Einstein's life on sentence strips. Post them on a bulletin board to create a time line of Einstein's life.

ALBERT EINSTEIN

Name ____

Launch this Web site: http://www.geocities.com/CapeCanaveral/Lab/3555/

Directions: Click the link **To main Index** and then **Who was Albert Einstein really?**. Follow the arrows to learn about Albert Einstein from childhood to adulthood. Answer the questions.

About Albert Einstein's Childhood

1. At playing which musical instrument did Einstein excel before the age of five? ______________
2. What did Albert Einstein think of school? ______________________________

   ____
3. Was he a good student? ______________________________

About Einstein's Early Career

4. What subjects did Einstein teach? ______________________________
5. What job did he have after teaching? ______________________________

About Einstein's First Breakthrough

6. In what city was Einstein living when he finished his general theory of relativity? ______________

   ____

About Einstein's Second Marriage

7. Who was Einstein's second wife? ______________________________
8. What unusual occurrence proved Einstein's general theory of relativity? ______________

   ____

About Einstein's Final Years

9. Besides physics, what else was Einstein interested in? ______________________________

   ____
10. Why did Einstein write a letter to President Roosevelt? ______________________________

    ____

MARTIN LUTHER KING, JR.

Objective:

As leader of the Civil Rights era, Dr. King's involvement brought forth significant changes in the treatment of minority peoples. Students consider the unfair treatment minorities received and then create an "infowheel" of chronologically ordered events that took place in Dr. King's life.

Materials Needed:

- one copy of page 54 for each student
- one paper plate for each student
- one brad paper fastener for each student
- writing paper

Focus Web Site—Destination URLs:

The Dr. King Time Line Page
http://buckman.pps.k12.or.us/room100/timeline/kingframe.html

About This Site: This student-created site teaches others about King's life. There are 32 date links allowing viewers to read about specific events throughout his life. Viewers learn a great deal of information about King and view illustrations created by the students.

Alternative Web Sites:

Martin Luther King, Jr.
http://www.seatimes.com/mlk/index.html

Dr. Martin Luther King, Jr.: A Biographical Sketch
http://indigo.lib.lsu.edu/lib/chem/display/srs218.html

Dr. Martin Luther King, Jr. (sponsored by the National Civil Rights Museum)
http://www.mecca.org/~crights/mlk.html

MARTIN LUTHER KING, JR. (cont.)

Pre-Internet Activity:

Ask the students if they have ever felt as if they were not being treated fairly. Have them share their experiences. Ask them what they wished had happened differently which would have made them feel as if they were being treated fairly. Explain that not so long ago, African Americans in the United States were treated quite differently from everyone else; they could not attend the same schools, drink from the same fountains, eat where they pleased in restaurants, etc. Tell the students that Martin Luther King, Jr., was a peaceful leader in gaining equality for African Americans and other minorities and that they will learn about important events from his life on the Internet.

Teaching the Lesson:

1. Distribute a copy of page 54 to each student. They should cut and secure the "infowheel" to the plate before exploring the Internet. Students may write directly on their wheels as they gather information or select six date links and write the date and event on a separate sheet of paper before transferring it to their wheels.

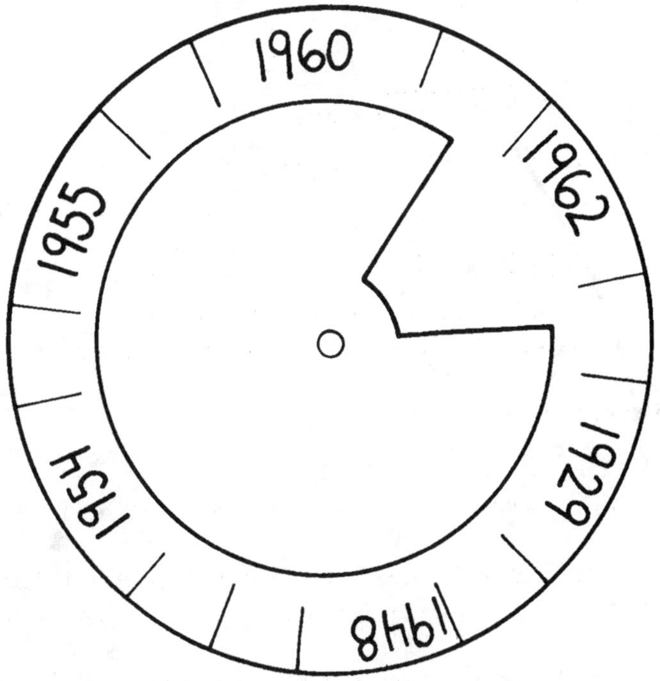

2. Allow small teams of students to access the Internet and gather the information. The dates on the wheels should follow in chronological order around the plates.

3. After everyone has completed the activity page, have each student choose a partner who was not in his or her Internet group. The partners share their infowheels with each other to learn more information about Dr. King from date links that they may not have accessed.

4. Following sharing time, have the students write a brief summary explaining what they learned about Dr. King.

MARTIN LUTHER KING, JR., INFOWHEEL

Name ____

Launch this Web site: http://buckman.pps.k12.or.us/room100/timeline/kingframe.html

Directions: Cut out the wheel below. Attach it to the center of a paper plate with a paper fastener. Link to one of the dates on the time line. Write the date on the outside edge of the paper plate. Write the event that occurred on this date in the space from the cutout section of the wheel. Illustrate the wheel.

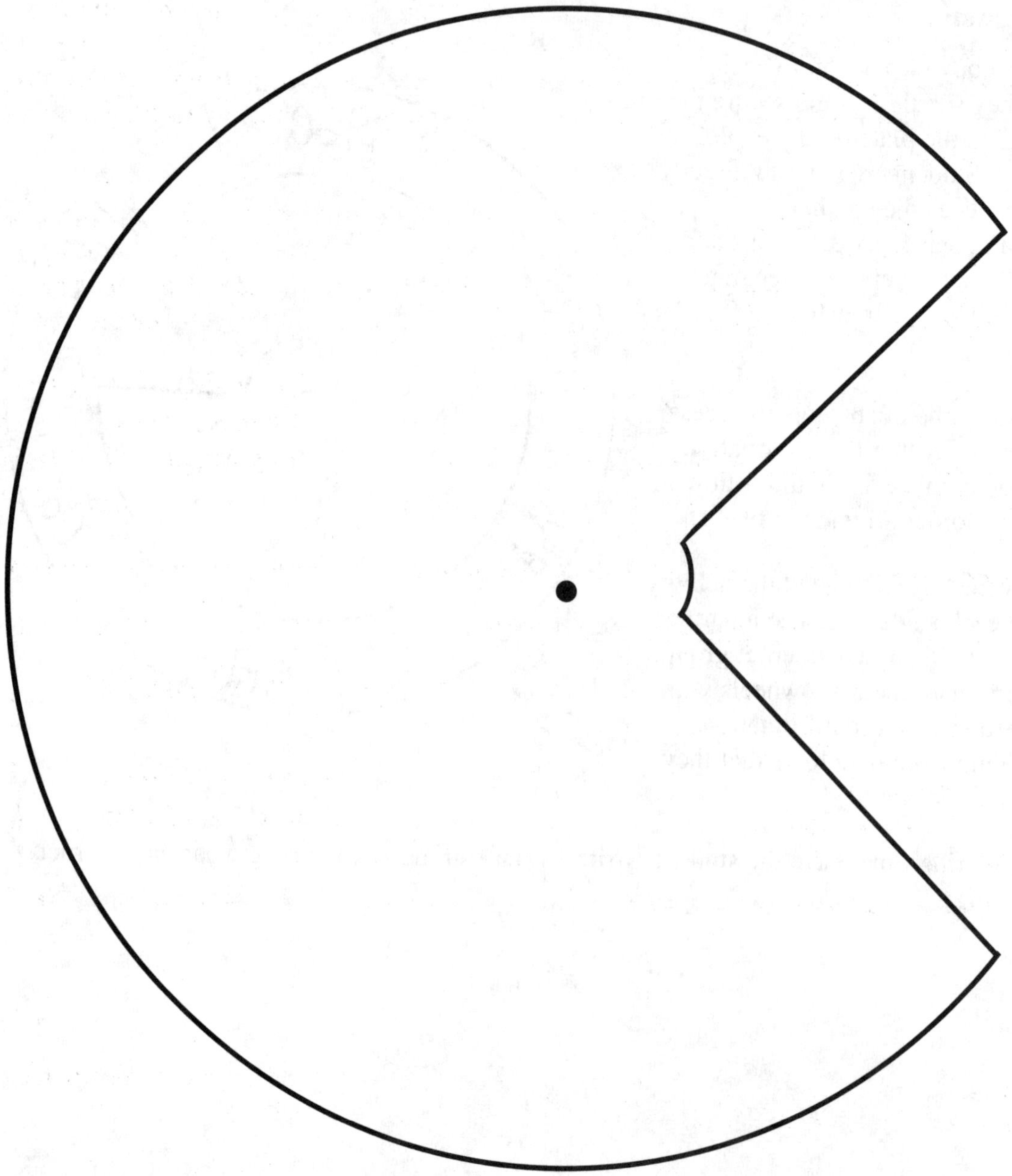

MARTIN LUTHER KING, JR. *(cont.)*

Extended Activities:

- Dr. King's most memorable speech was "I Have a Dream." Share this speech from a classroom resource book or by accessing either of the following Web sites.

  "I Have a Dream" Speech
  http://www.msstate.edu/Archives/History/USA/Afro-Amer/dream.king

  "I Have A Dream" by Martin Luther King, Jr.
  http://www.mecca.org/~crights/dream.html

  Assign small groups of students a brief section of the speech to read and summarize. Students share the meaning of their portion with the class in order from the beginning of the speech to the end. Have students consider something they feel strongly about and write a two-to-three-minute speech on the topic of their choice. Have them practice their speaking skills by reciting their speeches to the class.

- Discuss injustices that are occurring around the world today by sharing some newspaper articles describing worldwide events. Have the students consider how Dr. King would react to these events. Students work in small groups to consider a dilemma of their choice. They list changes they think Dr. King would have liked to have seen occur and possible solutions to the problem.

- The Civil Rights movement was a time of unrest in our nation's history, even though Dr. King supported peaceful demonstrations. Have the students work in teams of three or four to use more traditional means to research an event from the Civil Rights era. Then they prepare a short skit of this action and perform it for their classmates.*

Civil Rights Era Notable Events

Brown v. Board of Education	March on Washington, D.C.
bus boycotts	Watts riot
sit-ins	Civil Rights Act of 1964
freedom rides	Voting Rights Act of 1965

***Author's Note:** Use the activities from "Rosa Parks," pages 56 to 59, and the second extended activity of "Jackie Robinson" on page 63 to complement the third extended activity above.

ROSA PARKS

Objective:

As the "Pioneer of Civil Rights," Rosa Parks started the nation toward equality for all people. Students consider her act from a legal and human perspective as well as learn about Rosa's accomplishments and contributions to the Civil Rights effort.

Materials Needed:

- student survey from page 59 for each student
- dictionaries, reference materials
- chalkboard or chart paper
- one copy of page 58 for each student
- writing paper

Focus Web Site—Destination URLs:

Rosa Parks Biography
http://www.achievement.org/autodoc/page/par0bio-1

About This Site: Here students learn about the beginnings of the Civil Rights movement by reading about Rosa Parks and her brave resolution not to relinquish her bus seat. This site is most notable for its quotes spoken by Ms. Parks from an actual interview.

Alternative Web Sites:

Take a Stand: Rosa Parks
http://www.leap.yale.edu/lclc/town/stand/rosa.html

40 years ago, Rosa Parks made history
http://www.spub.ksu.edu/issues/v100/FA/n070/cam-parks-edwards.html

Rosa Parks
http://www.neco.org/rosaparks.html

Rosa Parks: The Woman Who Changed a Nation
http://www.grandtimes.com/rosa.html

ROSA PARKS *(cont.)*

Pre-Internet Activity:

Have the students fill out the questionnaire on page 59. When they've completed this task, poll the class to determine how they answered the third question. What if the students thought a law was unjust? What if they didn't know they were breaking the law? In either scenario, do the students think they should be punished? Explain that they will visit a Web site about a lady, Rosa Parks, who felt obliged to break a law to make a point and was punished for her actions.

Teaching the Lesson:

1. Provide students with some vocabulary background before visiting this Web site. Post the following terms on the chalkboard or on a chart. Assign groups of students to investigate their meanings and write the definitions or explanations next to the words.

segregation	Ku Klux Klan	flog
freedom	lynch	peonage
Civil Rights	NAACP	murder

2. Distribute a copy of page 58 to each student. Launch the focus Web site as a class. Read the information on the Web pages, and then have students answer the questions on the activity sheet.

3. Lead a discussion about the legal/human perspectives of Rosa Parks' actions and consequences.

4. Write each of the following questions on the chalkboard. Students write their responses on a sheet of paper.

   › Do you think Rosa Parks should have been put in jail simply for refusing to give up a seat on the bus? Why or why not?
   › Was the law she broke fair to everyone? Why or why not?
   › Against whom did it discriminate? Why?
   › Was her punishment suitable for what she did? Explain.
   › Should Rosa have done what she did? Explain.
   › Was Rosa Parks dangerous? Explain.

   Discuss the students' answers as a class. Poll the class from question one to see how many students thought jail was necessary. If students say no, remind them that she did in fact break a law, a punishable act. What do the students think should have happened to her? Continue the discussion by reviewing the students' answers to the questions.

   Have students review their questionnaires from the pre-Internet activity. Using a pen, students circle items for which they may have changed their minds and write a brief explanation for the change on the backside of the page or on a separate sheet of paper.

ROSA PARKS: AN ACT OF DEFIANCE

Name ____

Launch this Web site: http://www.achievement.org/autodoc/page/par0bio-1

Directions: Read the information at this Web site. Consider the questions below and write your responses.

1. Why was Rosa Parks arrested on December 1, 1955? ______________________
____

2. Do you think she should have been arrested? Why or why not? ______________________
____

3. Why is this considered the beginning of the modern Civil Rights movement? ______________________
____

4. Why were there so few opportunities available to Rosa in the early 1900's? ______________________
____

5. How did her single act of defiance change that? ______________________
____

6. Why was Rosa not afraid to do what she did? ______________________
____

7. What three notable events occurred as a result of her actions? ______________________
____
____

8. List two accomplishments Rosa achieved in her life. ______________________
____

9. Do you think Rosa will ever reach complete happiness? Why or why not? ______________________
____
____

10. List three cities in Alabama where Rosa lived. ______________________
____

ROSA PARKS *(cont.)*

Extended Activity:

Discuss Rosa Parks' view on happiness. She says in order to be happy, you have to "have everything that you need and everything that you want." Do the students agree with her philosophy? Have the students write and illustrate a poem expressing what happiness means to them. Combine them into one book entitled "Poems of Happiness."

Name: ____

Student Survey

Directions: Place an X in the box if you agree with the statement.

- ❑ All laws are fair to everyone.
- ❑ People should never break the law.
- ❑ Everyone who breaks the law should be punished.
- ❑ Punishments always fit the crime.
- ❑ People should stand up for what they believe in.
- ❑ Peaceful lawbreakers are just as dangerous as violent lawbreakers.

JACKIE ROBINSON

Objective:

Students consider Jackie's difficult responsibility of being the first modern-day African American major league baseball player and compare his professional accomplishments to those of their favorite sports stars. Then they create true and false questions about Jackie and test their knowledge in a friendly game of "Jackie Robinson Grand Slam."

Materials Needed:

- chalkboard
- one copy of page 62 for each student
- writing paper
- five copies of the baseball bat pattern from page 61 for each pair of students

Focus Web Site—Destination URLs:

The Jackie Robinson Society
http://www.utexas.edu/students/jackie/

About This Site: Students may select from numerous related links to articles of interest about this famous baseball player who "broke the color barrier."

Alternative Web Sites:

Jackie Robinson: Breaking Barriers
http://www.majorleaguebaseball.com/jackie/

Stealing Home: A Tribute to Jackie Robinson
http://www.sound.net/~vivian/jackie.html

The Official Site of Jackie Robinson
http://www.jackie42.com/

Life Hero of the Week: Jackie Robinson
http://www.pathfinder.com/@@jMr0jwYAxuCeQu@g/Life/heroes/how/robinson.html

JACKIE ROBINSON *(cont.)*

Pre-Internet Activity

Have the students list some of their favorite professional sports heroes and tell why they admire them so much. List each celebrity under his or her appropriate sport heading on the chalkboard. Circle the names of those who are minority figures. Explain that some writers agree that without the efforts of Jackie Robinson, those people wouldn't have had an opportunity to play professional sports. Tell the students that they will have a chance to research on the Internet how Jackie Robinson paved the way for future minority players as well as aided the Civil Rights effort.

Teaching the Lesson:

1. Using the lists the students generated from the pre-Internet activity, discuss the contributions those athletes have made to their sports. How would sports be different if minorities were denied the right to play professionally?

2. The authors of the focus Web site deem Jackie Robinson as the "greatest athlete of the 20th century." What do the students think of this honor? Whom would they consider the greatest present-day athlete?

3. Distribute a copy of page 62 to each student. Students work as a class or in small groups to access the destination URL and complete the activity page.

4. After everyone has finished, have the students give the reasons why the authors consider Jackie Robinson to be the "greatest athlete of the 20th century." Have the students changed their minds regarding whom they would select since step 2? Have the students write an essay comparing Jackie Robinson's professional accomplishments to those of a sports figure of their choosing.

5. Revisit the focus Web site as a class. Demonstrate how to write a true sentence from the information as well as change a factual statement into a false one. Give each pair of students five copies of the baseball bat pattern below. Allow the partners to access the focus Web site and write five true or false statements about Jackie Robinson. They write a "T" or "F" in the tip of the bat handle to indicate whether the sentence is true or false.

6. Use the facts and falsehoods to play "Jackie Robinson Grand Slam" either as a class or in small groups. The class or groups must first divide into two teams. One person is the caller. Each team member has a turn to state whether the sentence is true or false. After four correct answers, the team scores a "home run" and one point. The team loses its turn after three "strikes" or incorrect answers. Then the next team members take turns answering true or false. After all the statements have been posed, the teams tally their scores.

A NEW STAR IN THE BIG LEAGUES

Name ____

Launch this Web site: http://www.utexas.edu/students/jackie/

Directions: Arrow down the page. Click on the link "**Read the Jackie Robinson Society article, 'Athlete of the Century'**." Read the information and answer the questions.

1. Jackie was full of "firsts." Besides being the first African American major league baseball player, list four other "first" African American achievements he made. ____________________

2. Jackie's stardom was not easily achieved. List two hurdles he had to clear as he entered a world where no African American had been before. ____________________

3. Give an example of how Jackie's actions helped the Civil Rights movement. ____________________

4. Name two ways Jackie's achievements are honored today. ____________________

5. In what other sports did Jackie excel? ____________________

6. Why didn't he play them professionally? ____________________

7. Do you agree or disagree that Jackie Robinson was the "greatest athlete of the 20th century"? Why? ____________________

JACKIE ROBINSON (cont.)

Extended Activities:

- As a class, re-access the focus Web site and select the link "A collection of quotes by and about Jackie Robinson." Read what others have had to say about Jackie Robinson as well as what he has said about himself. Have the students use these quotes to assign personality traits to Jackie. Was he humble? Aggressive? Timid? Have the students write a simple poem defining his character traits and the reasons for them.

- Jackie Robinson did his part to support the Civil Rights movement. As a class, access the link "An exclusive look at Jackie Robinson's involvement in the Civil Rights Movement." Discuss his involvement and the actions he took in the fight for equality for all. Have the class consider the advantages Jackie had over some other African American Civil Rights supporters that enabled him to encourage changes.

- Students may have an interest in discovering additional minority "barrier breakers" in other sports. Allow interested students to access the link "A look at African Americans who were barrier breakers in other sports." They research a sport of their choosing and write a report on paper cut and decorated to resemble a piece of athletic equipment from their respective sports. Post the students' work on a bulletin board entitled "The First Score."

- Have the students work in pairs to create a mock television interview between a news reporter and Jackie Robinson. Students may select any event from Jackie's life on which to base a dialog. They perform their skits for the class.

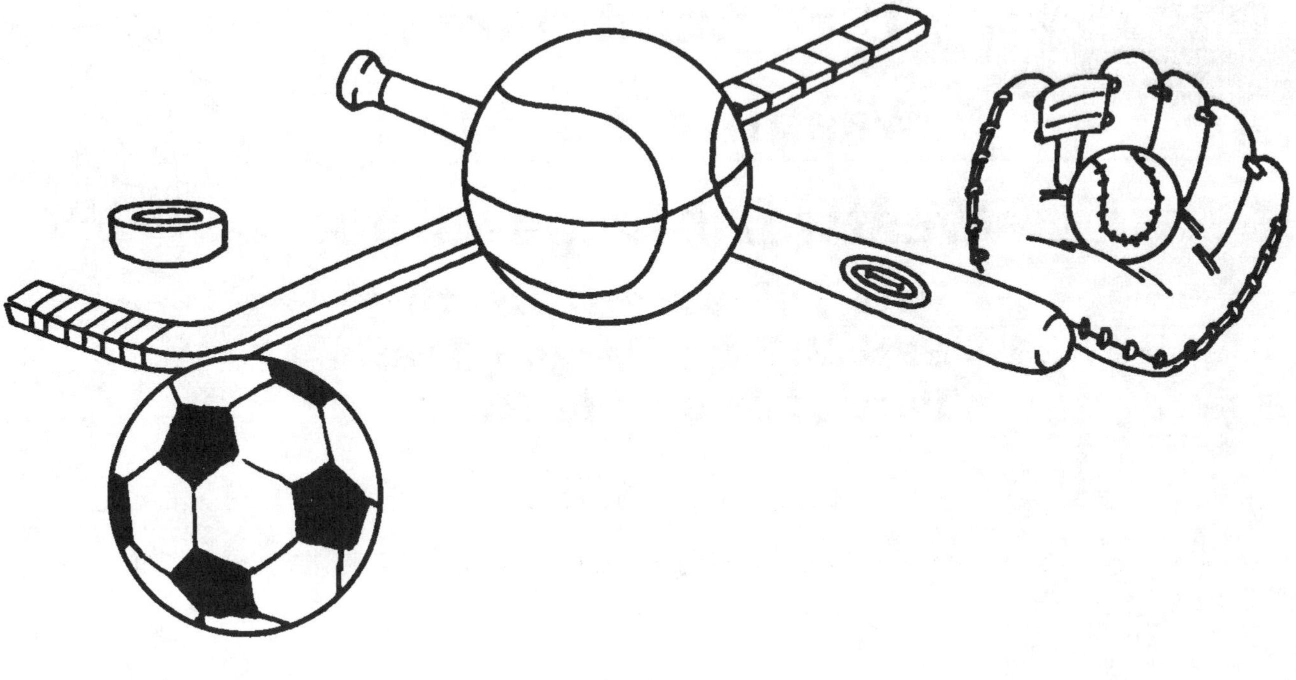

In the U.S.A.

"What would our nation be without this great land of ours?"

—Ronald Reagan

Students discover the history and land of the United States of America with Internet activities focused on the following topics:

Immigration

U.S. Geography

U.S. Landmarks

Washington, D.C.

Westward Expansion:

Part 1: Manifest Destiny
Part 2: The Oregon Trail
Part 3: The Gold Rush

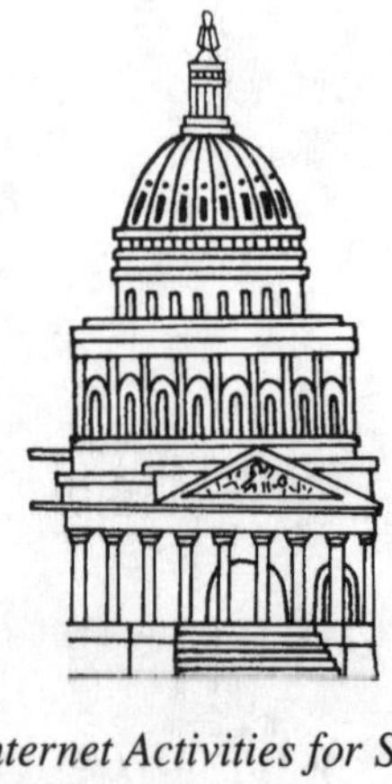
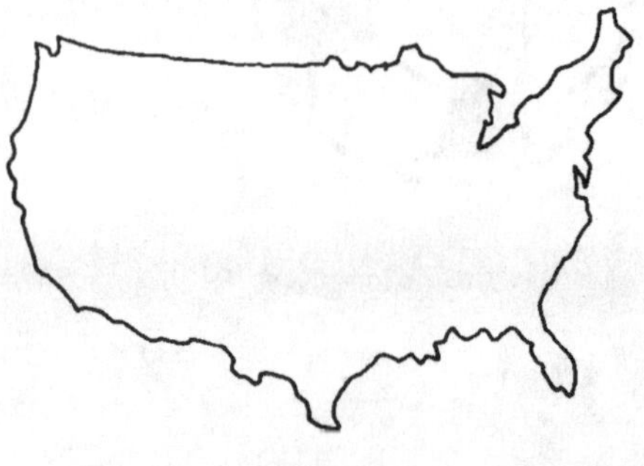

IMMIGRATION

Objective:

Since its birth as an English colony, people have been immigrating to the lands that make up the United States from all over the world. Students compare the differences immigrants of the 1600s faced versus immigrants of the 1800s and even those of today. They organize the information according to years and then write a journal entry for each era of immigration.

Materials Needed:

- chalkboard or chart
- drawing paper
- 13 copies of page 67 or one for each group
- four large note cards for each group
- writing paper

Focus Web Site—Destination URLs:

The American Immigration Home Page
http://www.bergen.org/AAST/Projects/Immigration/index.html

About This Site: Here students will find a complete listing of various topics related to immigration. The information is divided into four time-related chronologies beginning in 1607 and continuing through the present.

Alternative Web Sites:

Ethnic Mosaic of the Quad Cities
http://www.augustana.edu/library/ethnic/

New York at the Turn of the Century
http://lcweb2.loc.gov/ammem/papr/nyc.html

IMMIGRATION *(cont.)*

Pre-Internet Activity:

Have the students share their ancestral heritages (German, Greek, Russian, Cuban, etc.) and, if they know, the approximate year their ancestors first arrived in the United States. Write the ethnic groups the students mention on the chalkboard or on a chart. Assign each student or pair of students a different country for which to draw a flag so that as many countries' flags as possible are represented. Suspend them from the ceiling or post them in the hall with the heading "Arrived from Many Nations."

Teaching the Lesson:

1. Have the students think of reasons why people would want to leave their native countries and emmigrate to the United States. Then have them consider how immigrants arrived when our nation was first born and compare that to how they think immigrants of today arrive.

2. Divide the class into up to thirteen groups, one for each category listed at the focus Web site. Write one of the following category titles on the top line of each research guide.

   - ➪ Reasons for immigration
   - ➪ Who were/are the immigrants to the U.S.?
   - ➪ Peaks/waves of immigrants
   - ➪ Methods of transportation and ports of arrival
   - ➪ Process of entering the U.S.
   - ➪ Destination/places where they settled
   - ➪ Treatment/reception by other Americans
   - ➪ Effects/impact on America (positive and negative)
   - ➪ Opportunities for and success of immigrants
   - ➪ Assimilation? If so, to what degree?
   - ➪ What did/do immigrants find distinctive about America?
   - ➪ Legal vs. illegal immigrants
   - ➪ Laws restricting immigration

3. Give each group a copy of page 67, each with a different category to research. Launch the Web site with the class. Have the students speculate as to why there is a gap in the information (from 1924 to 1968). Explain that while researching their topic, they should only include the most important details on their papers. Allow the groups to retrieve their information off the Internet. They share what they learned about their category with the class.

4. Have the groups list the category title, years, and information from each era onto four large note cards. Combine the era cards to make study guides about particular eras of immigration to the United States. Place them at a center for students to review during their free time. Play "That Era in History" Trivia by writing the four eras on the chalkboard and then asking questions about the categories to teams of students. The students answer in which era those events took place.

5. Have the teams work together to write four journal entries as if they were an immigrant during each of the four eras. Combine them according to era to make four journal books. Send them home with a different student each afternoon so that all the students may share their work with their parents.

A COUNTRY OF MANY NATIONS

Name ____

Launch this Web site: http://www.bergen.org/AAST/Projects/Immigration/index.html

Directions: Find the category link written on the line below. Link to each era by clicking the years links. Fill in the lines with information about each era.

Category ____

Years 1607–1830 ____

____

____

____

____

Years 1830–1890 ____

____

____

____

____

Years 1890–1924 ____

____

____

____

____

Years 1968 to Present ____

____

____

____

____

IMMIGRATION *(cont.)*

Extended Activities:

- Ellis Island played an important role in the immigration process during our nation's history. These Web sites provide an inside look at this now historical site once filled with eager, yet apprehensive, newcomers to the United States.

  Ellis Island
  http://www.i-channel.com/ellis/index.html

  Ellis Island
  http://www.ellisisland.org/

  New York, NY, Ellis Island—Immigration: 1900–1920
  http://cmpl.ucr.edu/exhibitions/immigration_id.html

  Ellis Island Photos by Phillip Buehler
  http://www.icgnet.com/users/phil/ruins/ellis/index.html

  Have the students experience Ellis Island firsthand by having "Coming to America" day. Prior to the big event, write new names on cards, one for each student. Assign an area in the classroom to be the "deportation area." Students must first submit a simple entry application including their names, country of origin, and reasons for wanting to immigrate to the United States. Line up the students outside the classroom door. They attempt to gain entry at Ellis Island (with you acting as the immigration official). When students first arrive, tape a new name to their clothes. Speaking in jibberish, assign them a place to stand in the room. You reserve the right to "deport" anyone who is acting up, argumentative, or suspicious looking. Once everyone has entered, begin immigration proceedings. First, they must pass the test. Begin in one area and ask obscure, ridiculous, or historical questions of each student. Students answering incorrectly must go to the deportation area. Finally comes the medical exam. Pretend to check the students' eyes, tongues, and ears. Anyone failing the medical exam must also go to the deportation area. After all the students have had their chance to pass through Ellis Island, discuss their emotions and concerns as well as the fairness of the proceedings. Relate these feelings to how real immigrants might have felt coming into Ellis Island.

- Value the ethnic diversity of the class by having a cultural feast. Each family supplies an ethnic dish to share with the class. Invite parents and relatives to share in the celebration as well. Provide ethnic games to play, if possible. Set a time and date, and let the celebration begin!

U.S. GEOGRAPHY

Objective:

In part one of "Teaching the Lesson," students use traditional means to organize the details on one of seven regions of the United States and then reference a national park or geographic land form in that region. In part two, students apply their latitude and longitude skills to identify cities on a blank U.S. map.

Materials Needed:

- enlarge regions from page 71 onto poster board, chart, or bulletin board paper
- atlases, color relief maps of the United States, individual state maps
- large note cards
- one copy of page 72 for each student

Focus Web Sites—Destination URLs:

Yahoo!
http://www.yahoo.com

Geographic Name Server
http://www.mit.edu:8001/geo

About These Sites: Students use the Yahoo! search engine to research a national park or geographic feature from a particular region of the United States. The latter site provides latitude and longitude data to complete the second half of the activity.

Alternative Web Sites:

Students may search the Internet database with a search engine of their choosing (see list on page 10).

U.S. Census Bureau
http://www.census.gov/cgi-bin/gazetteer

ETAK Guide
http://www.etakguide.com/
(Arrow down the page, enter the city and state, and then select **<Draw Map>**. Along the top line of the map, select the button for **<Lat/Long>** and then click on the map.)

U.S. GEOGRAPHY *(cont.)*

Part One: Teaching the Lesson:

1. Enlarge each region of the United States from page 71 onto poster board or a large sheet of chart or bulletin board paper.

2. Divide the class into seven teams, one to research each region of the United States.

3. Students use atlases, color relief maps, and individual state maps to label the states and their capitals. They also mark major mountain ranges, deserts, rivers, lakes, swamps, marshes, etc. onto their enlarged region map. Finally, students identify and label three national parks in their region.

4. Have the students launch their favorite search engine home page (Yahoo! is recommended) and type in the name of a national park (e.g., Yosemite, Mammoth Cave) or geographic feature (e.g., Niagara Falls) from their region to search. They select an appropriate Web site from which to gather information about this area of interest and record the information onto a large note card.

5. Students share their research with the class, using their geographic region maps and Internet research.

6. Post the students' region maps and Internet research in the hall with the heading "Around the U.S.A."

Part Two: Teaching the Lesson:

1. Following a lesson on the concept of latitude and longitude, have students practice marking locations on a blank U.S. map. Distribute a copy of page 72 to each student. They launch the Web site and mark the locations of the cities on the map.

2. For additional practice, have the students use a U.S. map showing latitude and longitude lines to select two cities they think have about the same latitude and two others that share the same longitude. Have them access the focus Web site to discover if they were correct.

3. As a class, select a city in Alaska and compare its latitude to the cities on the activity page. Likewise, select a city in Hawaii to compare its longitude.

4. (Optional) When the students access the focus Web site to complete the activity page, have them record the populations of the cities as well. The students use this information to create a bar graph.

5. (Optional) Students can see the view of two of the cities listed on the activity page (Jacksonville and Wichita) as they appear from outer space! Link to the Web site listed below, select **latitude, longitude and altitude** and then **list of cities**. In addition to viewing two of the cities from the activity page, students can observe the similarities and differences between a city in the mountains and one in the desert; a city near the ocean and one in the plains, etc.

   Earth and Moon Viewer
   http://www.fourmilab.ch/earthview/vplanet.html

U.S. GEOGRAPHY *(cont.)*

Use these U.S. regions with part one from "Teaching the Lesson" on page 70.

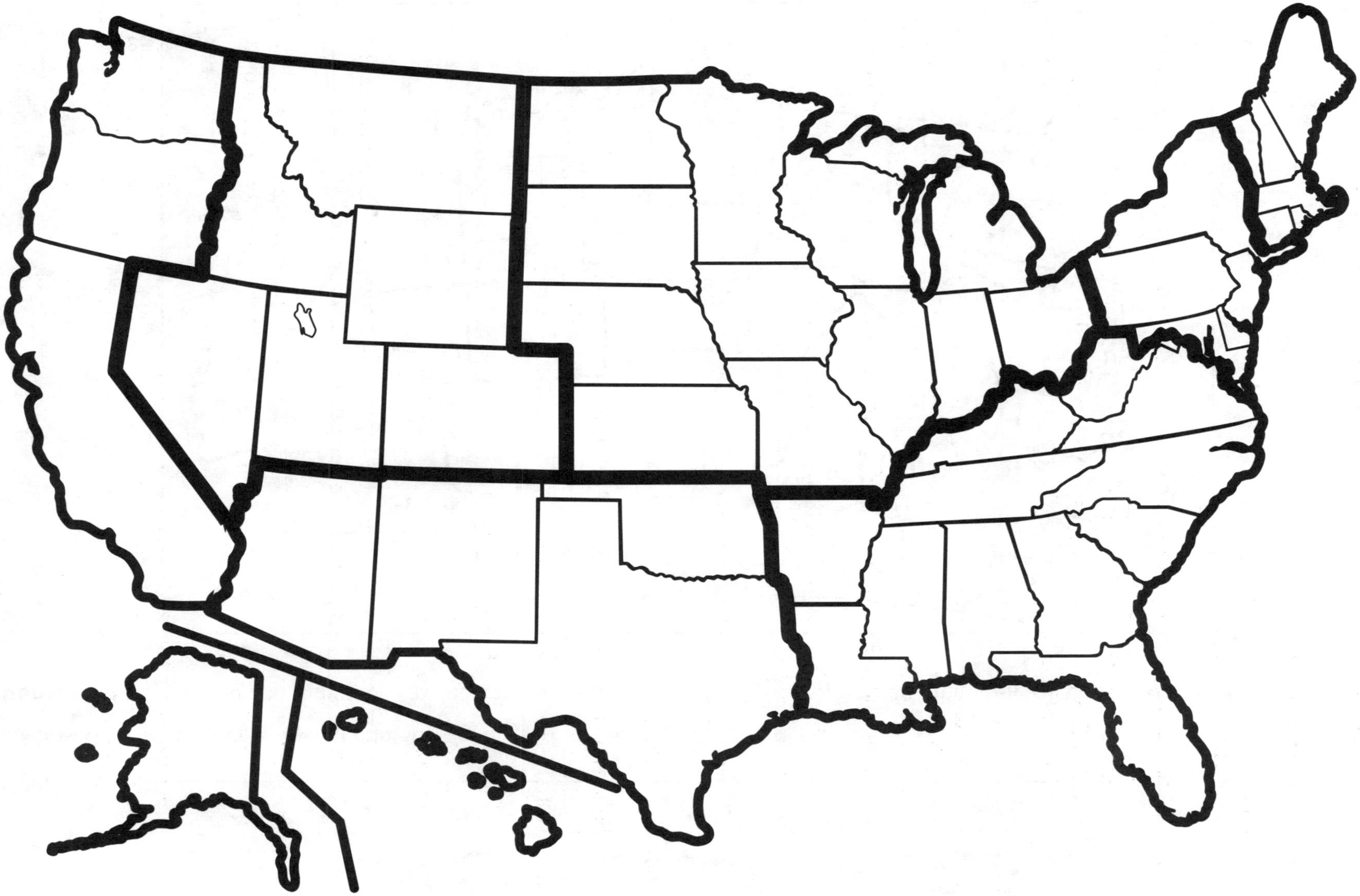

YOU ARE HERE

Name ______________________________

Launch this Web site: http://www.mit.edu:8001/geo

Directions: Find the latitude and longitude (in degrees) of each U.S. city below. Estimate and mark their locations on the map.

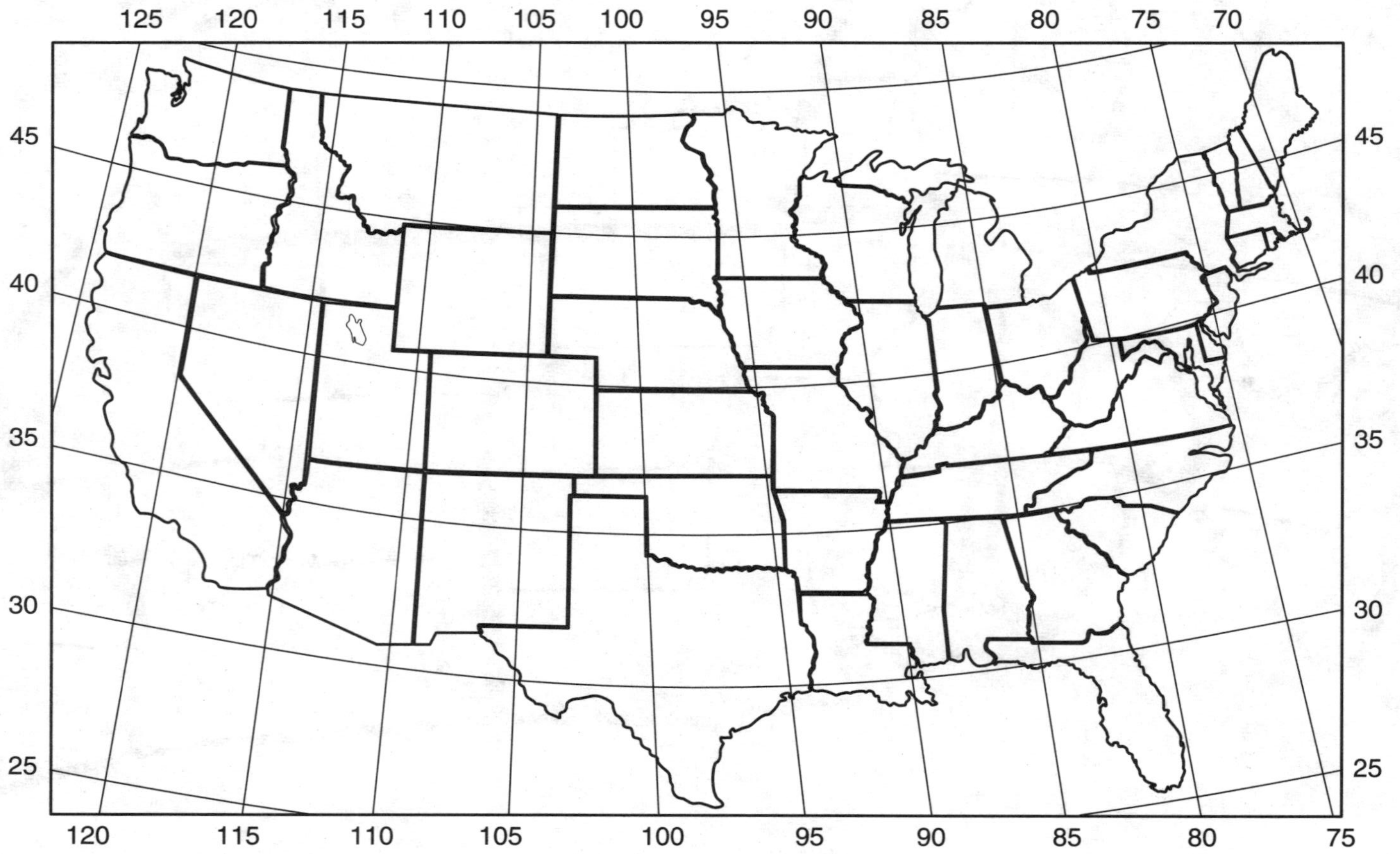

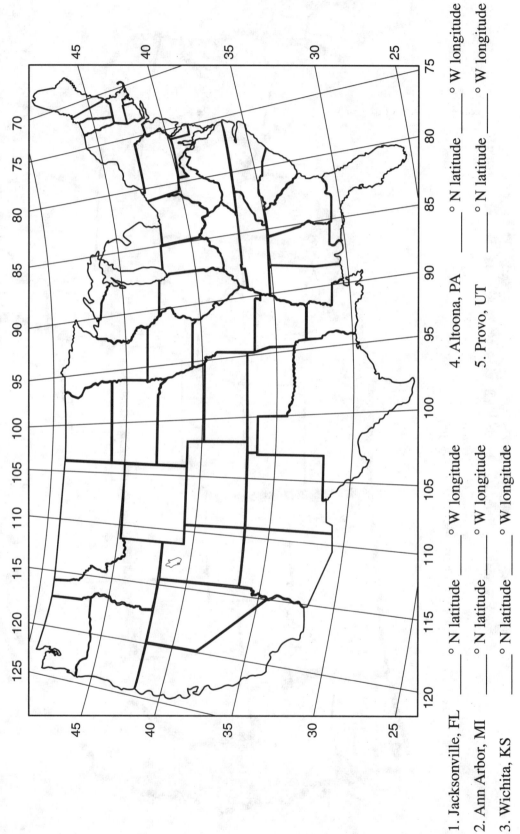

1. Jacksonville, FL _____° N latitude _____° W longitude
2. Ann Arbor, MI _____° N latitude _____° W longitude
3. Wichita, KS _____° N latitude _____° W longitude
4. Altoona, PA _____° N latitude _____° W longitude
5. Provo, UT _____° N latitude _____° W longitude

U.S. GEOGRAPHY *(cont.)*

Extended Activities:

- Students can practice using a map legend to measure distances from their hometown to another city of their choice across the United States. Then they check their calculations by launching this Web site, typing in the two cities, and submitting their entries. The computer will return with the proper distance.

  How Far Is It?
  http://www.indo.com/distance

- Have the students keep searching on the Internet and searching maps to discover little known trivia facts about the geography of the United States. For example . . .
  - › what is the northernmost state of the 48 contiguous states? (MN)
  - › true or false? Las Vegas is west of the easternmost tip of California. (True)
  - › which states border the Gulf of Mexico? (TX, LA, MS, AL, FL)

- If the class welcomes more global comparisons, assign pairs of students to gather information about one of the many countries at the following Web site. Display the students' data in a grid for easy comparison.

  Country Profiles
  http://home.worldonline.nl/~quark/ixprof.html

Country	Capital	Area (sq. mi.)	Population	Yearly Growth
Australia	Canberra	2,967,970	18,260,863	.99%
Bangladesh	Dhaka	55,599	123,062,800	1.85%
Cameroon	Yaoundé	183,569	14,261,557	2.89
Poland	Warsaw	120,727	38,642,565	.14%
U.S.A.	Washington, D.C.	3,618,773	262,755,270	1.02%

- How well do the students know the shapes and contours around the globe? Check out these images from Space Shuttle missions (along with a clue to its identity) and try to guess the location of each particular formation around the world.

  Geography from Space
  http://ceps.nasm.edu:2020/GAW/GFSintro.html

- Students can test their knowledge of world geography by playing the online GeoBee Quiz at

  nationalgeographic.com GeoBee Quiz
  http://www.nationalgeographic.com/features/97/geobee/

U.S. LANDMARKS

Objective:

Students share their travel adventures with the class and then research a particular landmark from one of the fifty states. They use their information to create a collage poster advertising and telling about their curious structure.

Materials Needed:

- U.S. atlas or individual state maps
- one copy of page 76 for each pair of students
- one twelve-by-eighteen-inch sheet of drawing paper for each pair
- colorful construction paper
- various art supplies to create a collage (yarn, fuzzy balls, tinfoil, toothpicks, craft sticks, pipe cleaners, etc.)

Focus Web Site—Destination URLs:

Yahoo!
http://www.yahoo.com

About This Site: For referencing specific landmarks, students may choose to use this search engine or one of the others listed on page 10.

Alternative Web Sites:

Where would you like to go?
http://www.ehnr.state.nc.us/EHNR/files/usa.htm
(Click a state from the map and then **Tourism Information**.)

Yahoo: Top: Regional: U.S. States
http://www.yahoo.com/Regional/U_S_States/
(Click a state name and then **Travel**.)

Suggested Landmarks to Research

The Alamo (TX)
The Astrodome (TX)
The Blowing Rock (NC)
The Brooklyn Bridge (NY)
Chimney Rock (NE)
Devil's Tower (WY)
Graceland (TN)
Independence Rock (WY)
The Mark Twain House (MO)
Monticello (VA)
Mount Rushmore (SD)
Mount Vernon (NY)
The Octagon House (any)
The Seattle Space Needle (WA)
The St. Louis Arch (MO)
Stone Mountain (GA)

U.S. LANDMARKS *(cont.)*

Pre-Internet Activity:

Lead a discussion about the definition of a landmark (*a specific or unique object that identifies a particular location*). Give examples of landmarks in your area. Have the students share a favorite travel spot their family likes to visit when they take a family vacation. They tell the state to which they travel and some landmarks or tourist spots they see. Explain that they will have an opportunity to visit other landmarks on the Internet.

Teaching the Lesson:

1. Have the students work with a partner. The teams reference a U.S. atlas or individual state map. They use the map key to identify three to five landmarks or points of interest in that state they would like to investigate on the Internet and rank them in order from most to least interesting. (Or you may assign specific landmarks for the students to research on the Internet—see a suggested list on page 74.)

2. Distribute a copy of the landmark research guide from page 76 to each team. They launch their favorite search engine (Yahoo! is recommended), type in the name of the landmark they ranked as most interesting and then complete the research guide. If no information about their particular landmark is available, they may elect to use a different search engine, one of the alternative Web sites listed on page 10, or try referencing one of the other landmarks they identified from the atlas.

3. Students create a poster of the landmark they researched on a twelve-by-eighteen-inch sheet of drawing paper. They tear colorful construction paper into the shape of the state where this landmark is found and then use various art supplies to create a collage image of the landmark on one half of the paper. (No pencils, markers, or crayons allowed!) Then they write a summary of the information from their research guides to place on the second half of the paper next to their collage.

4. Post the students' work on a bulletin board or in the hallway with the title "A Site Worth Seeing!"

Extended Activities:

- Students further investigate tourist oddities in the state where their landmark is located and then create a travel brochure for that state.

- Students design and create a picture postcard of the landmark they researched. Place them around an enlarged U.S. map and attach a length of yarn from the postcard to the location on the map where each landmark can be found.

HOW CURIOUS!

U.S. LANDMARK RESEARCH GUIDE

Name ____

Launch this Web site: http://www.yahoo.com

Directions: Type in the name of the landmark you wish to reference and click **<Search>**. Select an appropriate Web site from which to gather the information below. Use additional paper, if necessary.

Name of landmark ____

City and state where it is located ____

Physical description ____

____

____

Historical information ____

____

____

How it got its name ____

____

____

Reasons to visit it ____

____

____

Sketch an illustration of it.

WASHINGTON, D.C.

Objective:

Students apply mapping skills to place a monument located in Washington, D.C., on a classroom map of the Mall area. They research their monument and provide a drawing and information to accompany the map.

Materials Needed:

- enlarge map of the Mall and surrounding area on poster board (see page 81)
- name of seven monuments written on note cards (see pre-Internet activity)
- seven copies of page 79, one for each group
- seven three-by-five-inch note cards
- seven additional note cards
- construction paper

Focus Web Site—Destination URLs:

The Washington, D.C. Fun and Recreation Page
http://www.his.com/~matson/index.html

About This Site: A little bit of history and a lot of fun are awaiting students at this Web site. Choose to read up on the buildings and structures that make the city so grand, or find out what Washingtonians do for fun and games around the town and surrounding countryside.

Alternative Web Sites:

City Beautiful: The 1901 Plan for Washington, D.C.
http://xroads.virginia.edu/~CAP/CITYBEAUTIFUL/dchome.html

The White House
http://www.whitehouse.gov/WH/Welcome.html

Welcome to the White House for Kids
http://www.whitehouse.gov/WH/kids/html/kidshome.html

WASHINGTON, D.C. *(cont.)*

Pre-Internet Activity:

Enlarge the map of the Mall (label only the Capitol Building and Smithsonian Castle) onto a sheet of poster board. Display it along with the names of seven monuments (with numbers) located in Washington, D.C.: (1) The Vietnam Veterans Memorial, (2) Arlington National Cemetery, (3) The Jefferson Memorial, (4) The Lincoln Memorial, (5) The Marine Corps War Memorial, (6) The Roosevelt Memorial, and (7) The Washington Monument. Have them speculate about the purpose of each monument. Explain to the students that they will have an opportunity to research each monument and discover where it is located on the map of the D.C. area.

Teaching the Lesson:

1. Divide the class into seven groups, one to research each monument. Assign the groups a monument to research by randomly distributing the cards to the groups.

2. Distribute a copy of page 79 to each group. Allow the groups to access the Internet, gather their information, and mark the location of their monument by writing the number on the Mall map. (The Marine Corps War Memorial is located near Arlington National Cemetery, and the Roosevelt Memorial is in West Potomac Park on the Tidal Basin.)

3. Students each transfer their sketch from the research guide onto a three-by-five-inch note card and cut it out around its outline. They secure it next to the location they marked on the map by folding the bottom edge of the picture back and gluing the tab to the poster board. Then they summarize the information they learned on an additional note card, including the name of the monument and the number. (Each monument on the map has a number next to it and a corresponding number on the card that gives details about it.)

4. Secure all the cards to one sheet of construction paper.

5. Display the completed three-dimensional Washington, D.C. map and cards in the library or on a table in the front office.

Extended Activities:

- Students may elect to create a simple three-dimensional model of their monument instead of simply using a paper drawing. Supply the students with the materials they need to complete this task. Follow the steps above to complete the map.

- Have the students reflect on their knowledge of American history to design and create a model of an original monument. They make a sketch or three-dimensional image of the monument and write a summary of its purpose, following the research guide on page 79. Students share their original monument with the class.

THE MONUMENTS OF WASHINGTON, D.C.

Name ____

Launch this Web site: http://www.his.com/~matson/index.html

Directions: Click on the monuments link. Select the name of the monument you will research. Complete the information below. Use additional paper if necessary.

Name of monument ____

Number on the card __________ Year it was erected or dedicated ______________________

Purpose of the monument ____

____

____

____

A little bit of history ____

____

____

____

Draw a picture of what this monument looks like.

Click on the **<u>downtown area and Mall area</u>** link. Write the number of the monument on the map in the classroom.

WASHINGTON, D.C. *(cont.)*

More D.C. Links:

Students can have their fingers on the pulse of the nation by clicking on this site to get in touch with Congress. Find out what's happening today in the House and the Senate, or find out who your Congress members are and e-mail them with a valid concern or compliment.

Congress.Org
http://207.168.215.81/

Complement a study of specific sites in Washington by visiting these Web sites with the class.

The United States Capitol Exhibit
http://lcweb.loc.gov/exhibits/us.capitol/s0.html

United States Capitol
http://www.aoc.gov/

Welcome to Washington, D.C.
http://www.ppsa.com/ppsa/graphics/t15/t15a.html

Arlington National Cemetery
http://xroads.virginia.edu/~CAP/ARLINGTON/arlington.html

The Smithsonian
http://www.si.edu/newstart.htm

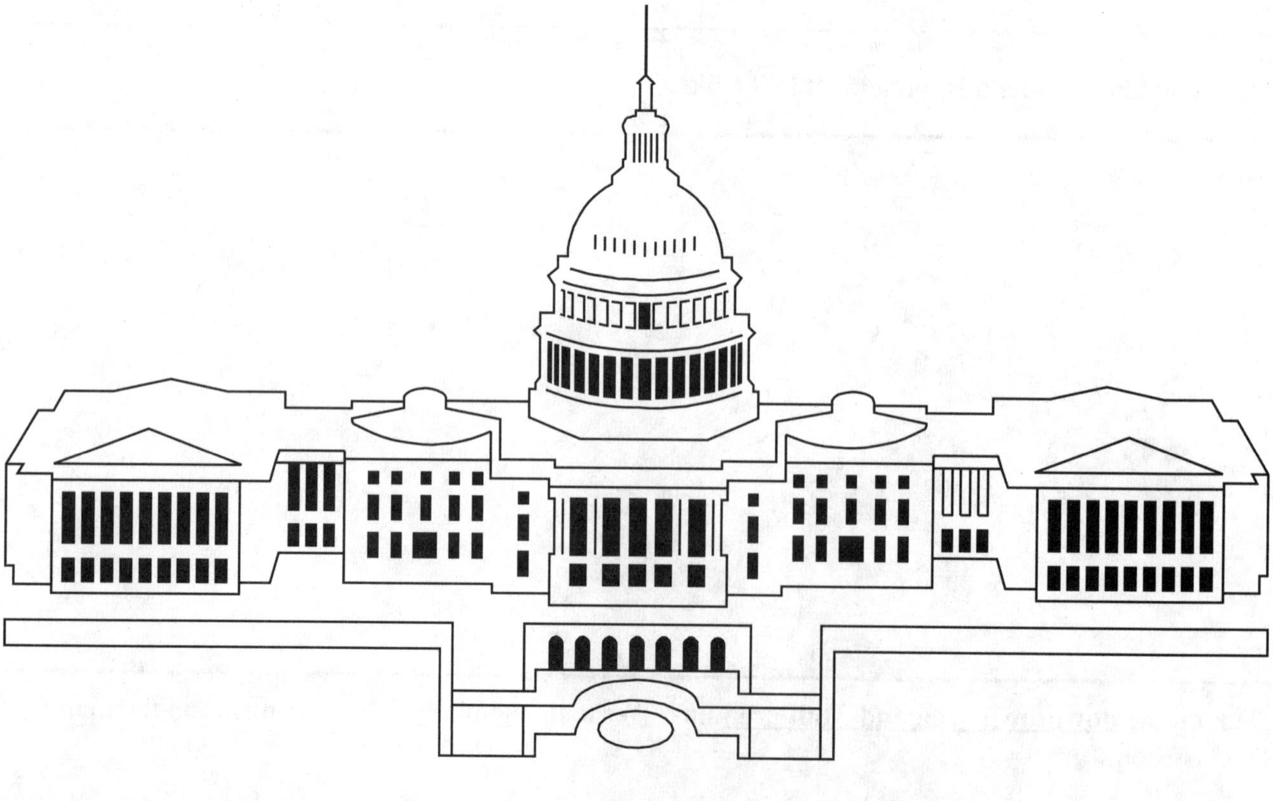

WASHINGTON, D.C. *(cont.)*

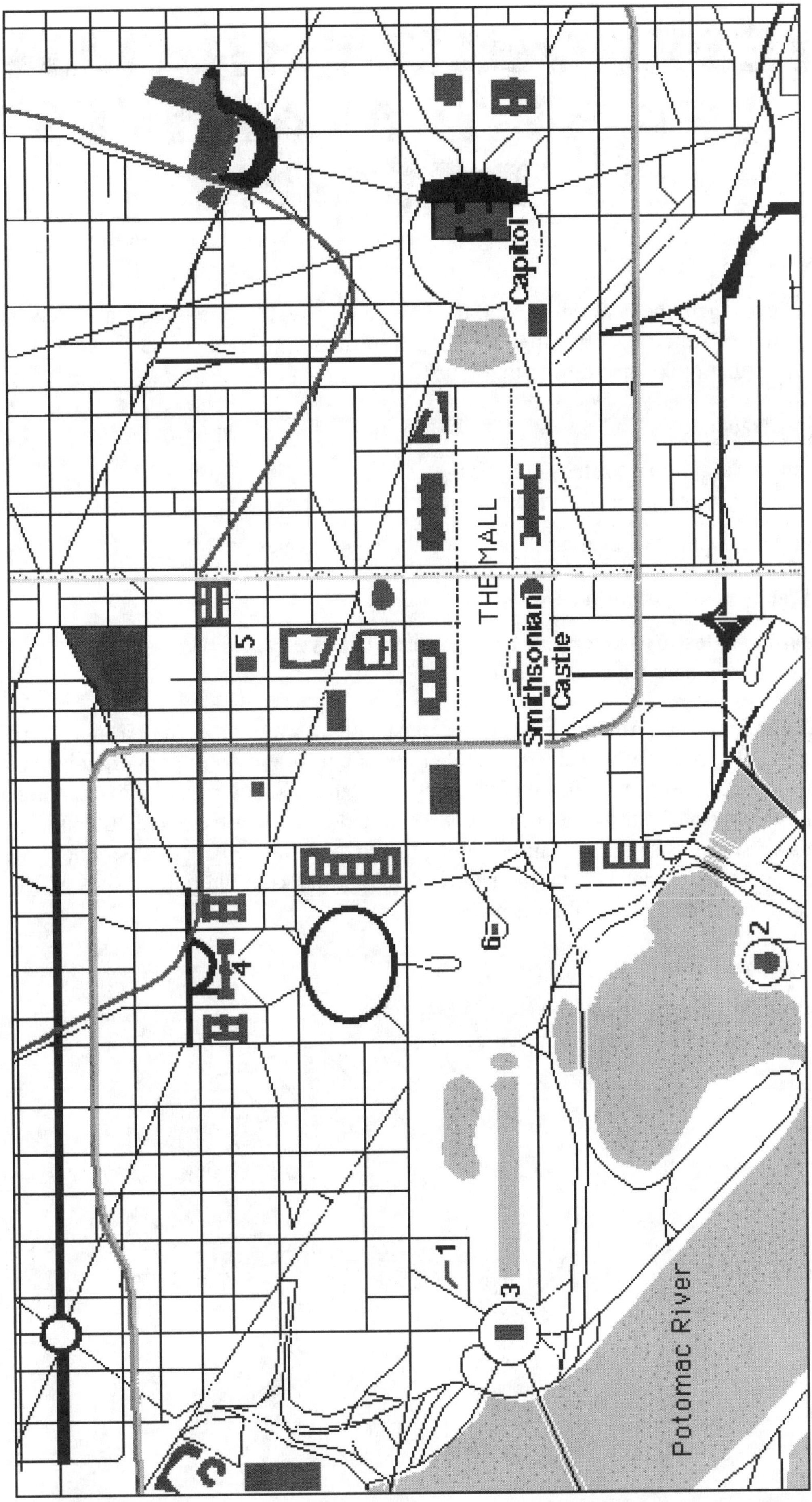

WESTWARD EXPANSION, PART 1: MANIFEST DESTINY

Objective:

Students investigate the histories behind the land in the West before these states became part of the United States of America. Then they use their information to write an 1800s style newspaper story about events that took place during that time.

Materials Needed:

- map of the original thirteen colonies
- nine copies of page 84
- parchment paper (if available) or plain white copy paper

Focus Web Site—Destination URLs:

Manifest Destiny: American Expansion in the West
http://garnet.acns.fsu.edu/~rbe6966/

About This Site: America's westward expansion is simply too large a topic to fit on one Web page. The maker of this site has categorized the information to help organize students' study of this subject. Students focus on one category, states, as they research the historical importance of individual states during the movement west. Other categories include books, pioneers/traders/settlers, relations with Mexico, and Native Americans. Each category includes a brief description and several links to related Web pages or alternative sites which the students select to gather additional information.

Alternative Web Sites:

Manifest Destiny: How the Rest Was Won
http://members.aol.com/htmpro/index.htm

Westward Expansion, Part 1: Manifest Destiny *(cont.)*

Pre-Internet Activity:

Post a map of the original thirteen colonies. Explain that although we associate the colonies with their respective state outlines of today, in actuality the states expanded from their easternmost tips all the way to the Mississippi River. After the colonists gained freedom from Britain, officials secured the states' boundaries as we see them today and left the remaining lands west to the Mississippi as territories for later development. As early explorers brought back information about the land west of the Mississippi, leaders of our new nation began to see the benefits of encompassing this land within the boundaries of the United States. *Manifest Destiny* was the theory by which the United States should naturally expand to its far western reaches (or to the Pacific Ocean). With Jefferson's acquisition of the Louisiana Purchase in 1803, people fled from overcrowded, dirty cities to start anew in the clean, untouched soils of the American West. (*The United States had acquired all of the land we know as today's U.S. boundaries by 1853.*) Explain to the students that they will have a chance to research some western states' histories before they were actually part of the United States.

Teaching the Lesson:

1. Divide the class into up to nine groups, one for each state referenced at this Web site. Write the names of the following states on each of the groups' activity pages: California, Colorado, Idaho, Kansas, New Mexico, Oregon, South Dakota, Texas, and Utah.

2. Launch the focus Web site as a class. Read the introductory paragraphs and discuss the author's meaning of his three tips: being careful of bias, using additional resources, and relying on reputable links and Web sites.

3. Arrow down the page. Read the category titles and discuss the kinds of information the students think they would find if they were to visit the links in these categories. Explain that some state details suggest linking to some of these sites as part of the state history. Students who have such a state may try those links after they have completed the activity page.

4. Distribute a copy of page 84 to each research team. Demonstrate how the students are to find their state, read the list of links, and then select a suitable site to visit. They should spend a few minutes reading the information and then fill in some information on their papers. They may always arrow back and select an alternative link from their state's category if they feel they may not be able to find the information at the Web page link they selected.

5. When all the groups have finished researching, have them review their information and then create a newspaper story related to their state's history. Students write on parchment paper, if available, including a bold headline and black marker drawings to accompany their stories. Or students may type their articles in a word processing or desktop publishing program and print them on parchment paper after final edits have been made.

THE STATES BEFORE THEY WERE STATES

Name ____

Launch this Web site: http://garnet.acns.fsu.edu/~rbe6966/

Directions: The western states were not always states. Learn about the history of these areas during the time of American expansion westward. Arrow down to the "states" category. Select a link from the list under the state below. Read the information and fill in the blanks. Use additional paper when necessary.

State: ____

Historical points of interest ____

____

____

Important people and their involvement ____

____

____

Important cities or towns and their history ____

____

____

Famous events or notable stories ____

____

____

Other interesting information ____

____

____

WESTWARD EXPANSION, PART 1: MANIFEST DESTINY *(cont.)*

Extended Activities:

- Have the students use more traditional means to research recent events in their state. They write and illustrate a "(Name of State) Then" and "(Name of State) Now" comparison poster by folding a large sheet of drawing paper in half. They write and illustrate events from the past on the left half and recent events on the right half. Post the students' artwork in the hall with the headline, "Past and Present."

- Revisit the focus Web site with the class each day to link to sites from the remaining categories. Have the students take notes of the day's information. Use their notes to make quiz questions for the end of the week or trivia cards for the students to quiz each other during their free time.

- Try the activities at this site to engage students in a simulation game about Manifest Destiny. The makers suggest its use with grades 7–9, but try reading their lesson and making adjustments suitable for your classroom.

  Teacher Talk:
  Manifest Destiny: Understanding Through Simulation
  http://education.indiana.edu/cas/tt/v2i2/manifest.html

WESTWARD EXPANSION, PART 2: THE OREGON TRAIL

Objective:

Students consider the means of travel across the Oregon Trail as they discover facts and details about the covered wagon.

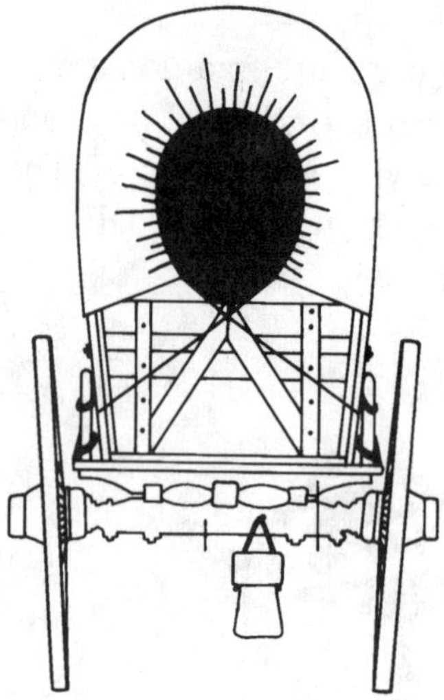

Materials Needed:

- drawing paper for each student
- one copy of page 88 for each student
- writing paper

Focus Web Site—Destination URLs:

The End of the Oregon Trail
http://www.teleport.com/~eotic/index.html

About This Site: This site hosts an abundance of links to information about the Oregon Trail Interpretive Center at the national historic site in Oregon City. Students may read about the history of the trail, the wagons pioneers used, or read some actual stories that took place on the Trail. Included, also, are links to a pioneer family of the month and information about African American pioneers to complement a study of minorities.

Alternative Web Sites:

The Oregon Trail
http://www.isu.edu/~trinmich/Oregontrail.html

Wagon Train of 1843
http://www.peak.org/~mransom/pioneers.html

The Oregon Trail: The Trail West
http://www.ukans.edu/kansas/seneca/oregon/mainpage.html

Teleport's Oregon Trail Roundup
http://www.teleport.com/features/orteail/links.html

Across the Plains in '64
http://208.206.78.232/daver/lsthand/atp/atp.html

In Search of the Oregon Trail: Trivia Questions
http://www.pbs.org/oregontrail/trivia.html

WESTWARD EXPANSION, PART 2: THE OREGON TRAIL *(cont.)*

Pre-Internet Activity:

Have the students list all the means of transportation that they can think of available in today's society. Then have them write a list of ways people could travel in the mid-1800s. Have the students imagine that they were part of a family who decided to move out West and brainstorm a list of dangers they might encounter along the way. (Students who frequently play *The Oregon Trail* should have valuable background knowledge from which to build.) Have the students draw a picture of themselves and their family members in a wagon as they journey West. They should pay particular attention to the wagon. Explain that the students will have a chance to research the details of the wagons on the Internet so that they may evaluate how closely they came to drawing an accurate portrayal in their pictures.

Teaching the Lesson:

1. Save the students' drawings for after their Internet visit. Have the students make educated guesses as to the actual size of the wagon box. They may demonstrate the dimensions using an area of the classroom floor as a guide.

2. Distribute a copy of page 88 to each student. Launch the Web site as a class and read the introduction. Explain that a living history museum is where the people act as if they really were living during a particular time in history (in this case, trail travelers in the mid-1800s).

3. Allow the students to work in small groups to access the **Wagons** link and complete the student activity page.

4. After everyone has had a turn, have the students evaluate their wagon drawings before they visit the Internet. Have the students share some inaccuracies in their drawings with the class. Each student writes how his or her wagon accurately and inaccurately represents an actual wagon from the mid-1800s.

5. Remind students that these wagons were ready for water as well as for land. Have them review the parts of the wagons and how they were prepared to cope with the elements.

6. Measure the approximate size of the wagon bed on the classroom floor (10 x 4 x 2 feet). Discuss how the western travelers must have carefully considered each item in their homes to determine what they would take and what they would leave. Have the students work with a partner to list five household items they absolutely could not do without (dolls and toys included). The groups share their lists with other students in the class.

WESTWARD IN A WAGON

Name ____

Launch this Web Site: http://www.teleport.com/~eotic/index.html

Directions: Click the **Wagons** link. Read the information. Label the parts of the wagon using the words below. Answer the questions.

driver's seat	wheel	bow	jockey box	brake lever
bonnet	bed	oxen	hub	

1. List the dimensions of a typical wagon.

   Length __________ Width __________ Depth __________

2. About how much did an empty wagon weigh? ______________________________
3. Why did the back flap overlap? ______________________________
4. List four valuable items that were usually attached to the wagon. ______________________________

   ____

5. Besides oxen, which two other kinds of animals might have led the family wagons? __________

   ____

WESTWARD EXPANSION, PART 2: THE OREGON TRAIL *(cont.)*

Extended Activities:

- Have the students use what they learned to create a model of a wagon using miscellaneous craft supplies. Display them in the media center for others to enjoy.

- Provide students with an order form below. Have them revisit the "Wagon" link from the focus Web site and arrow down to the bottom of the page to the listing of trail provisions. Show them how to divide (using a calculator, if necessary) to determine the amount each single item costs. Students log ten items on the paper as if making an order for themselves. After determining the individual costs, they may choose to order more or fewer than are listed at the Web site. Then they total their supply list by adding the "total" column.

Trail Provisions

Item	Cost per Item	Quantity	Total
Pepper	17 cents per pound	5 lbs.	.85
Candles	25 cents per pound	50 lbs.	$12.50

- Have pairs of students visit the **Stories** link and select from one of 52 articles related to the trail. They write a summary report in fewer than ten sentences and with two *ands* to share with the class.

Trail Provisions

	Item	Cost per Item	Quantity	Total
1.				
2.				
3.				
4.				
5.				
6.				
7.				
8.				
9.				
10.				
			Total Cost:	

WESTWARD EXPANSION, PART 3: THE GOLD RUSH

Objective:

Students consider the manner in which news traveled in the mid-1800s to make predictions about the news flurry about the gold rush. Then they apply sequencing skills to order the events in the history of the gold rush to make a time line.

Materials Needed:

- U. S. map (laptop desk maps, if available)
- writing paper
- one copy of page 92 for each student
- 12-by-18-inch drawing paper for each student

Focus Web Site—Destination URLs:

Virtual California Gold Country
http://www.malakoff.com/vcgc.htm

About This Site: Take a stroll down ol' Highway 49 and the history of the California gold rush. Read the news about some real-life mining camps or choose a biography of one of the many brave souls who battled the dangers for a chance to strike it rich!

Alternative Web Sites:

The Great American Gold Rush
http://www.acusd.edu/~jross/goldrush.html

The California Gold Rush
http://ceres.ca.gov/ceres/calweb/geology/goldrush.html

Memoir of the California Gold Rush as Told by Eugene Ring (1827–1912)
http://uts.cc.utexas.edu/~scring/index.html

WESTWARD EXPANSION, PART 3: THE GOLD RUSH *(cont.)*

Pre-Internet Activity:

Lead a discussion about how news travels to various parts of the country (or all over the world, for that matter!). How might its manner of travel have differed in the mid-1800s? Have the students use a U.S. map to estimate how a big news story originating in New York might have traveled to other parts of the country in 1850. They write their predictions on paper and then share their ideas with a group of up to five students. As a class, discuss the differences and similarities the students noted about each other's predictions. Tell the class that they will have a chance to use the Internet to read about how word of the discovery of gold in California traveled across the country.

Teaching the Lesson:

1. Distribute a copy of page 92 to each student. As a class, read the ten items on the page. Have the students make predictions about what happened first and last.

2. Assign pairs or groups of three to access the Internet and complete the activity page.

3. Distribute a 12-by-18-inch sheet of drawing paper to the students. They cut the items from the page into sentence strips and use them to make a time line on the drawing paper.

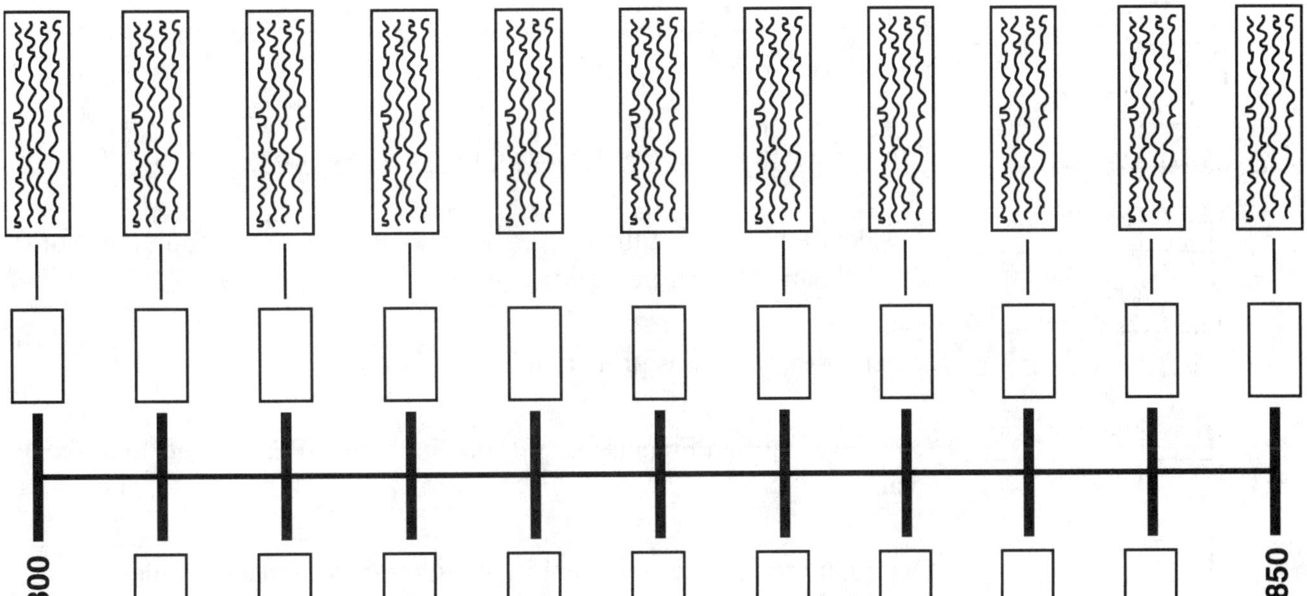

4. As a class, review the order in which word of this discovery reached various parts of the country. (San Fernando to San Francisco to Monterey to Hawaii to Oregon to Los Angeles to "The States") How can the students explain its haphazard trail?

5. Have the students use what they learned at the Web site to write an article for the local paper as if it is 1850 and they have just discovered gold in the playground of their very own school!

CALIFORNIA GOLD COUNTRY

Name ____

Launch this Web site: http://www.malakoff.com/vcgc.htm

Directions: Click the **Introduction** link. Read about the history of the California gold rush. Number these events in the order in which they occurred in the box to the left. Write the date the event occurred on the line.

☐ __________ News of the gold reached the Sandwich Islands (Hawaii).

☐ __________ An article telling of the gold discovery appeared in the St. Louis newspaper.

☐ __________ James W. Marshall discovered gold at Sutter's Sawmill.

☐ __________ The first '49ers arrived in California.

☐ __________ According to historians, gold mining began near the Spanish Mission of San Fernando.

☐ __________ Word of the gold discovery reached the people of Los Angeles.

☐ __________ President Polk verified the gold news in a report to the nation. His words set off a nationwide gold-seeking frenzy.

☐ __________ Sutter's discovery was printed in *The California*.

☐ __________ Gold fever hit San Francisco; everyone in the town had set off to strike it rich.

☐ __________ Don Francisco Lopez discovered gold in the San Fernando Valley.

WESTWARD EXPANSION, PART 3: THE GOLD RUSH *(cont.)*

Extended Activities:

- When word of gold first struck cities and towns in California, people fled their homes in search of treasure. But people in other parts of the country were skeptical until President Polk issued his proclamation. Then it seemed as if all the people were abandoning their homes to flock to California to find gold. Discuss the reasons for the people's skepticism and what changed their minds. How did the exaggerated tales coming from California fuel the fire? Have the students look through the local newspaper for a realistic story. Then they rewrite it, exaggerating some details to the point of near ludicrousness. Post the students' articles on a bulletin board entitled, "Now That's News!"

- Assign pairs of students to access the **Mining Camps** link and select a camp they would like to read about. They read about the camp and then prepare a short dialog that may have occurred between two camp members. They should include the details of the camp in their dialog.

- Students who are extremely fascinated with this time in our nation's history may also wish to link to the **Gold Rush Players** to read about some actual people who lived in the camps and mined for gold. Have them prepare a brief summary of a miner's life with the class and express his motivation for mining.

- Gold seekers didn't have fast-moving cars or airplanes to ride in to make a quick break for California. Have the students work as teams as they pretend to head west to gold country. (Students on the West Coast may work to reach diamond sites in the upper peninsula of Michigan.) Each group begins in its hometown. The groups roll two dice three times, adding the totals from each roll to determine the number of miles they travel each day. They plot their slow course on a U.S. map. Gold seekers will be determined to be the first in their class to reach the gold mines. Supply the winners with a small amount of gold-wrapped candy. Share a piece with everyone in the class for participating in the great gold rush!

MORE WESTWARD EXPANSION WEB SITES

For more enthusiastic students, assign them the task of referencing one of the following sites and gathering little known information about the Old West or a famous outlaw, gang, or lawman. Have them work in small groups to put on a Wild West skit to share the information they learned with the class.

The Trail of Tears
http://www.ngeorgia.com/history/nghisttt.shtml

Listing of Old West History Articles
http://www.historybuff.com/library/refwest.html

The Autobiography of Calamity Jane
http://www.geocities.com/Heartland/Acres/8427

The Notorious Clanton Gang
http://www.clantongang.com/

The Wild Wild West
http://www.gunslinger.com/west.html

My World

(MULTICULTURAL STUDIES)

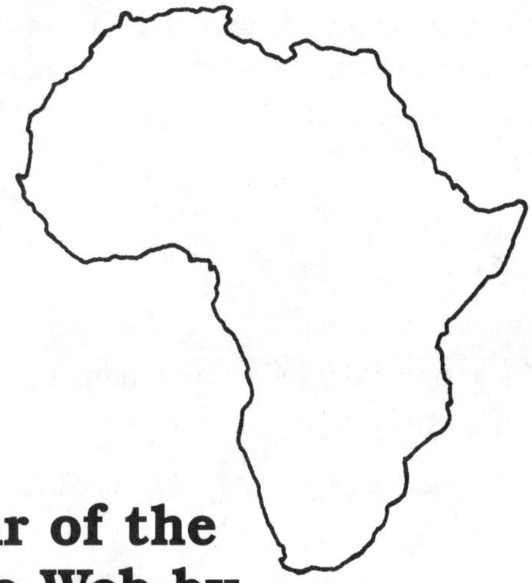

Take students on a tour of the world on the World Wide Web by visiting sites about the following countries:

Africa: On Safari

Canada

China

Greece

Russia

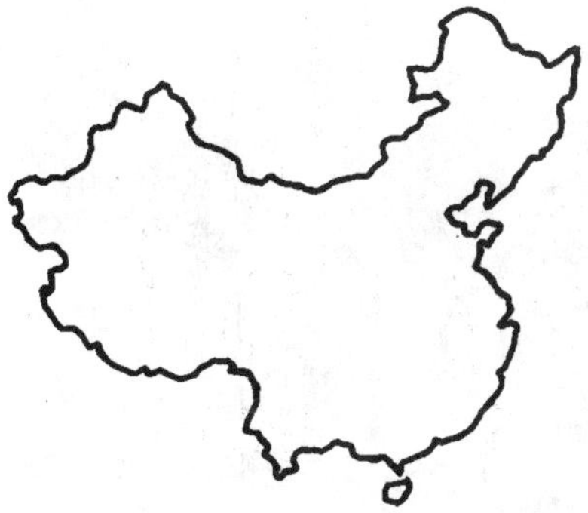

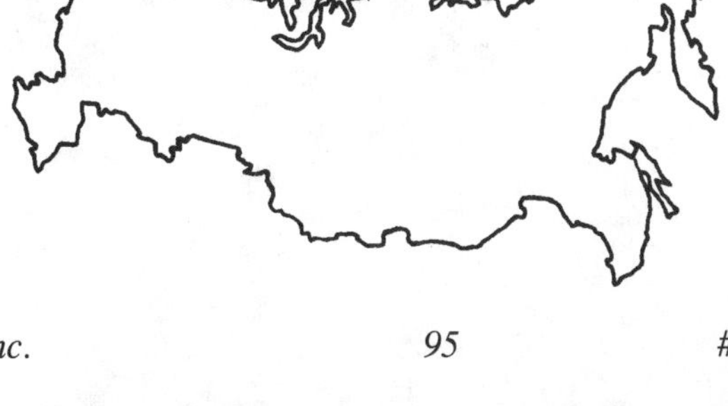

AFRICA: ON SAFARI

Objective:

The wilds of an African jungle are merely a click away when students don their pith helmets and travel to Okavango, a delta region of Botswana, where they track animals indigenous to this area. Then they research the animals and create their own set of mysterious tracks so others may go on Safari.

Materials Needed:

- map of the continent of Africa
- chalkboard
- world map
- one copy of the pith helmet pattern from page 98 for each student
- tagboard strip measuring about 2 by 26 inches for each student
- one copy of page 99 for each student
- note cards
- black construction paper (optional) and white construction paper

Focus Web Site—Destination URLs:

Okavango: Africa's Savage Oasis
http://www.nationalgeographic.com/features/96/okavango/index.html

About This Site: Sponsored by National Geographic, this site has everything ready to take students on a virtual safari in Botswana, Africa. This site is nearly entirely graphics and the pages take some time to download, but the imagery and accompanying information are well worth the wait.

Alternative Web Sites:

Africa: Kids Only
http://www.africaonline.com/AfricaOnline/coverkids.html

Africa Land
http://www.focusintl.com/afriland.htm

Africa Online
http://www.africaonline.com/

City.Net: Africa
http://city.net/regions/africa/

AFRICA: ON SAFARI (cont.)

Pre-Internet Activity:

Display a map of the continent of Africa. Have the students identify some countries with which they may be familiar and show their locations on the map. Have the students name some animals they might see if they were to go on an African safari. List them on the chalkboard. Explain that although we think of elephants as being from Africa, they, like much of the wildlife, are only found in specific regions, not over the entire continent. Tell the students that they will have a chance to track some animals on an African safari on the Internet in one specific location of Africa called Okavango.

Teaching the Lesson:

1. Review these geographic terms: delta, river, lake. Have the students define each term and give an example of each, using a world map. Explain that the region of Africa they will be visiting is part of a delta. They will learn more specific information when they visit the Web site.

2. What African safari would be complete without the appropriate gear? Have the students color and decorate the pith helmet outline from page 98. Secure it to a headband measuring 2 inches high by 26 inches long, and staple to fit around the students' heads.

3. Distribute a copy of page 99 to each student. As a class or in small groups, have the students follow the directions to complete the activity page. Students may need assistance using the map scale to complete questions 3 through 5.

4. Divide the class into six groups to further research the six animals whose tracks they identified: cheetah, wild dog, pangolin, lechwe, crocodile, and hippopotamus. The students write their information on a large note card or create a report in a word processing program. Then they make a long trail of tracks cut from black construction paper and glued to a strip of white construction paper measuring 18 by 6 inches. (Students may also simply draw the tracks onto the paper strip.) Post the students' tracks and information in the hallway with the title, "Mysterious Tracks." Challenge the students from other classes as well as visitors to match the tracks with the correct African animal.

AFRICA: ON SAFARI *(cont.)*

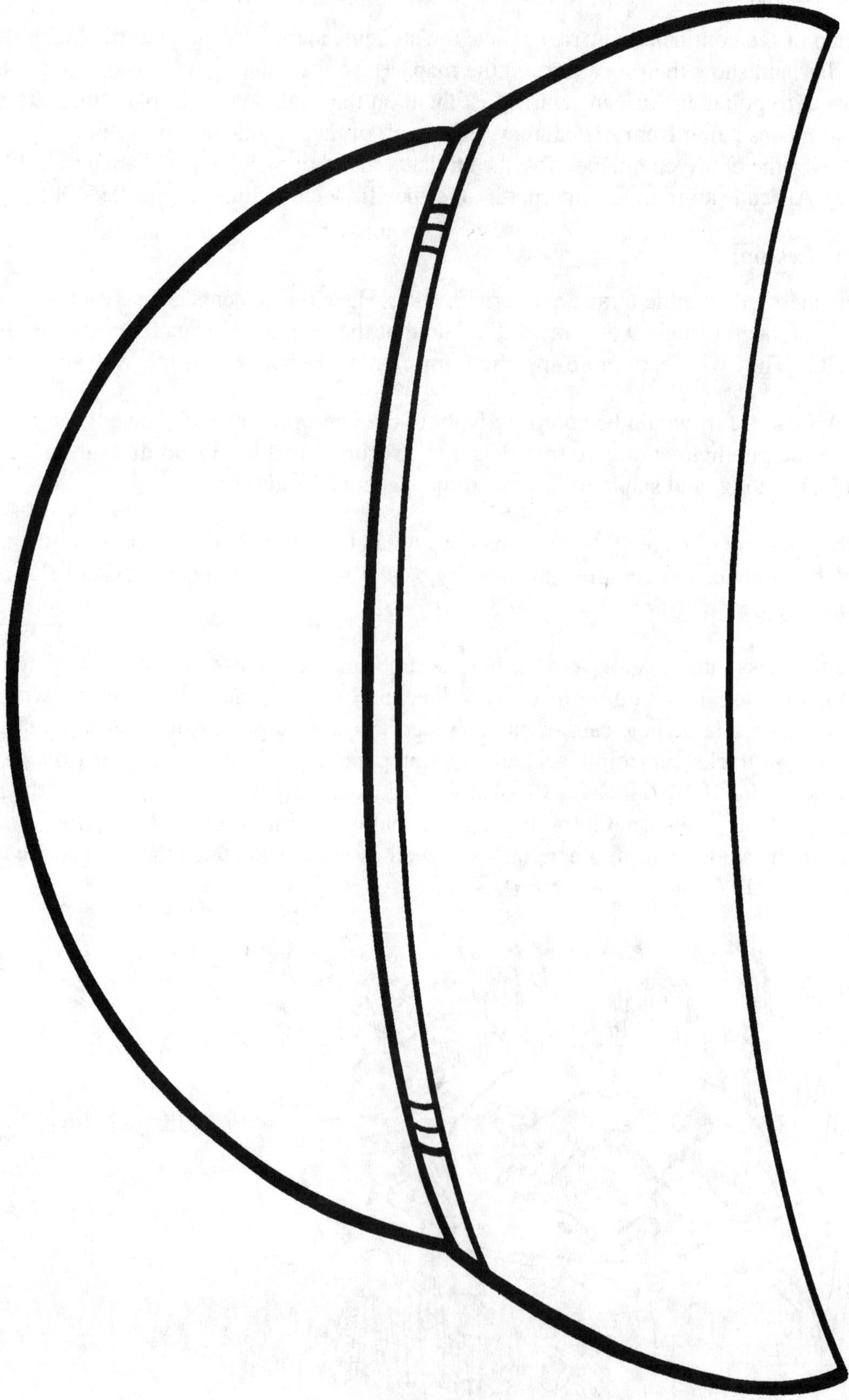

ON SAFARI IN OKAVANGO

Name ____

Launch this Web site: http://www.nationalgeographic.com/features/96/okavango/index.html

Directions: Select the link "Track On" to discover your mission on this safari. Then click the "Map" link. Read the information and follow the links to complete this page.

1. In which African country is Okavango? ______________________________

2. How is the water here replenished? ______________________________

   ____

Click the map to the left of the information to see the area more clearly. Use the map scale to determine the approximate distances between these cities.

3. From Shakawe to Ncamaseri ______________________________

4. From Ncamaseri to Etsha ______________________________

5. From Etsha to Matlapaneng ______________________________

Click the <**Back**> arrow from the task bar. Now go to the **Field Reports**. Select the link to **Match the Tracks**. Try to match the tracks for each of the six animals. The computer will tell you when you're correct. When you identify the tracks, sketch them in the spaces below.

Cheetah	Pangolin	Lechwe

AFRICA: ON SAFARI *(cont.)*

Extended Activities:

- In addition to reporting on and marking the tracks of the animals on safari, students may download an outline of the animals to print and color. From the "Field Reports" link of the focus Web site, select "Sketchbook" to choose the animal to view as a black and white drawing. After printing and coloring the graphics, students may include them in their written reports. (See step 4 from page 97.)

- Students may enjoy an authentic African tale on the Internet. This full-length story is available for pleasure reading complete with colorful illustrations. Spend oral reading time one day sharing this mesmerizing tale with the students.

  Tristan on Safari
  http://www.johnruss.com/bedtime/

- Students observe the animals on safari through faux binoculars. Encourage the students to view the world through this perspective by bringing in sets of binoculars clearly labeled with their names. Spend some time outdoors viewing wildlife (or still life) through the lenses, and then give students a copy of the pattern below to sketch their observations as seen through the binoculars. Post them on a bulletin board entitled "A Bird's-Eye View."

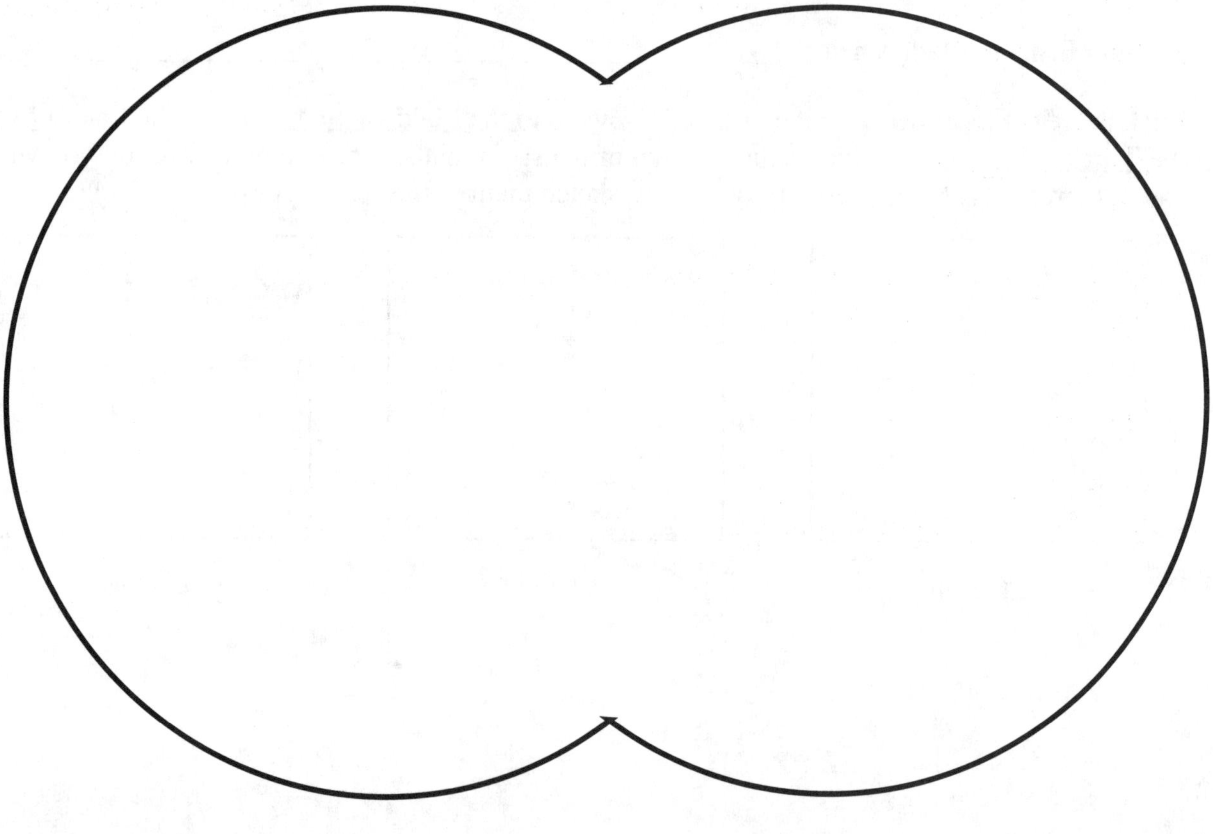

CANADA

Objective:

Maps are more than just lines and colors with city labels. After learning and applying the use of a pie chart, students gather important physical and demographic data from three different maps related to Canada's geography.

Materials Needed:

- physical map of the United States or the western hemisphere
- chalkboard
- one copy of page 103 for each student

Focus Web Site—Destination URLs:

Canadian Geographic Online
http://www.cangeo.ca/

About This Site: Go online to read the latest issue of *Canadian Geographic* magazine. Special features and stories about the past, present, and future will catch viewers up on Canada's news. Included, also, is a "Geo Map" feature depicting a host of geographic and demographic maps and charts from past issues.

Alternative Web Sites:

Great Canadian Parks
http://www.interlog.com/~parks/

British Columbia Ministry of Environment, Lands, and Parks
http://www.env.gov.bc.ca//

World Wildlife Fund Canada
http://www.wwfcanada.org/

Map of Canada (graphic only)
http://www.lib.utexas.edu/Libs/PCL/Map_collection/americas/Canada.GIF

CANADA *(cont.)*

Pre-Internet Activity:

Display a physical map of the United States or western hemisphere. Discuss how the information portrayed on this type of map differs from a typical map. Show the students how to determine where mountain ranges are located as well as water, flatlands, and other physical regions. Introduce the term "demographics." Explain that this word is used to identify human populations within a specific region. A demographic map or chart may depict the actual population, the number of nationalities represented in a specific population, the number of people who hold certain kinds of jobs, the ages of people living in specific regions, or similar statistics (numbers and ratios) about the population of a specific region. Explain to the students that they will visit a site about Canada where they will link to different kinds of maps displaying its physical regions and demographic regions.

Teaching the Lesson:

1. Have the students gather statistical demographic information concerning their classroom population and display the data on a chart or map. Poll the students to determine the number of families who own pets and the types of pets they have. List all the pets on the board and tally the total number of animals the students have at home. Explain that the best way to display this type of information is to represent the percentages of each type of pet on a pie chart. To determine the percentages of each animal, divide the total number of one animal by the total number of pets in all.

   Example: 32 cats ÷ 88 total pets = about .36 or 36%

   After compiling the data (all the percentages), draw a large circle on the board. Explain that the larger the percentage, the bigger the "piece of pie" that animal will represent. Divide the pie into approximate pieces to represent the appropriate percentages. Then demonstrate how to assign each pie piece a color to label the chart so people who read the chart know which percentage belongs to which animal (the chart key). Once the students understand the basic function of a pie chart, they are ready to go online and learn some physical and demographic data about Canada.

2. Distribute a copy of page 103 to each student. As a class or in small groups, have the students visit the Web site and complete the activity page.

3. Link to the remaining map links. Discuss the purpose of each type of map. Who do the students think would benefit from the information on each map? How is the information pertinent to everyday life? Why might it be important to know? Each map accompanied a past article in *Canadian Geographic*. Have the students work with a partner to brainstorm a possible title for the article.

THE GREAT LAND OF CANADA

Name ____

Launch this Web site: http://www.cangeo.ca/

Directions: Select the **Geo Maps** link. Arrow down the page to find the following map links. You will need to use the <**Back**> arrow from the task bar before selecting the next links. Use the information from the maps to answer the questions.

Map link: **Immigration to Canada**

1. From which top five countries did Canada's immigrants originate according to 1993 figures?

____

____

____

____

____

Map link: **Canada's Physical Makeup**

2. Complete the pie chart showing the percentages of the kinds of land in Canada. Assign each section a color. Label the land and appropriate pie piece to match.

Physical Land of Canada

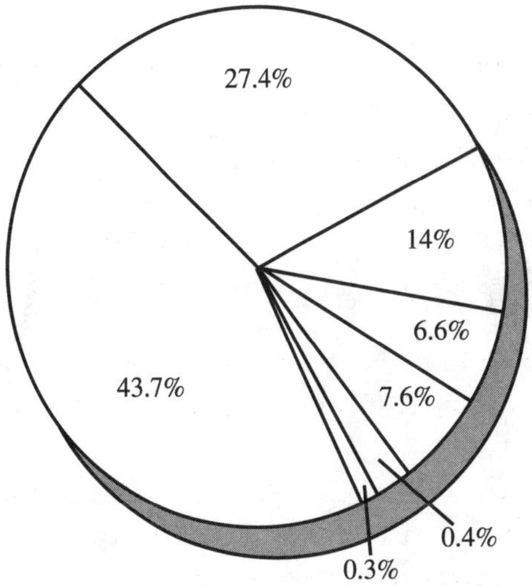

Map Key

- ☐ Arctic tundra and ice fields
- ☐ Agricultural land
- ☐ Open lands
- ☐ Urban areas
- ☐ Transportation
- ☐ Fresh water
- ☐ Facilities forests

Map link: **Travel to and from Canada**

3. List the top three countries people come from to tour Canada.

____

____

____

4. List the top three countries Canadians travel to.

____

____

____

CANADA *(cont.)*

Extended Activities:

- In addition to accessing the myriad maps and charts from the **Geo Maps** link, students may also read the special feature or other special article from the latest issue of *Canadian Geographic*. Topics include history and special events as well as other interesting reading about our neighbor to the north. Assign teams of two or three students the task of linking to a story and then creating a news report of the information they learned to share with the class.
- Have the students use their favorite search engine to link to informative Web sites about Canada. They work with a partner to read a site of interest and then select three facts about the country they think no one else would know. They write each fact on a red maple leaf cutout from the pattern below. Post them on a bulletin board entitled,"O Canada."
- Canada is divided into provinces: Alberta, British Columbia, Manitoba, New Brunswick, Newfoundland, Northwest Territories, Nova Scotia, Ontario, Québec, Saskatchewan, and the Yukon Territory. Display a country map of Canada and have the students identify each province. Then have them consider similarities and differences among Canadian provinces and the regions of the United States (see "In the U.S.A.: U.S. Geography," part 1, on page 70).

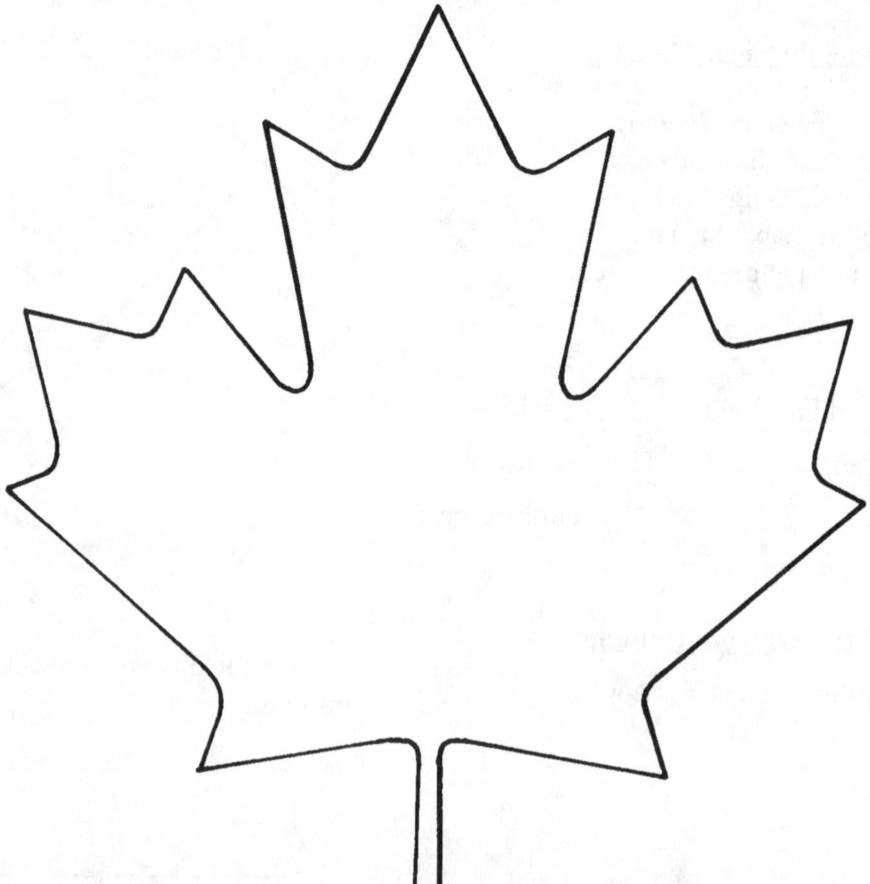

CHINA

Objective:

Students consider their reactions if they were to live in an unfamiliar country. Then they learn how the tendency for groups with common backgrounds to live together, excluding others, affects China's culture. They apply new vocabulary to their study of China and reference additional cultural and ethnic points of interest.

Materials Needed:

- chalkboard
- one copy of page 107 for each student
- large sheet of drawing paper
- additional drawing paper (optional)

Focus Web Site—Destination URLs:

China Today
http://www.chinatoday.com

About This Site: Seek the wonders of the Orient with this comprehensive Web site about China. Choose from a list of several category topics to investigate, including **Art and Entertainment**, **Culture and Ethnic**, **Travel and Tourism**, and many more. Numerous graphics accompany the text and invite the viewer to see them as full-screen images.

Alternative Web Sites:

Window on China
http://www.sinica.com/window-on-china/

China Vista
http://www.chinavista.com/

Map of China (graphic only)
http://www.lib.utexas.edu/Libs/PCL/Map_Collection/middle_east_and_asia/China_Admin_91.ipg

CHINA *(cont.)*

Pre-Internet Activity:

Review the students' nationalities. (See the pre-Internet activity from page 66.) Make a master list of them on the chalkboard. Discuss how the students, as Americans, would feel if they went to live in another country (Portugal, for example). What are some problems the students think might arise? What would help make their transition a little easier? Explain that when a large number of people immigrate to a specific country, they often form small communities of their own nationalities. Have the students work in small groups to brainstorm a list of pros and cons for this tactic. Have them share their ideas with the class. Explain to the students that in China a similar situation occurred, and they will have a chance to read about the diversity of populations inhabiting China.

Teaching the Lesson:

1. Post these terms and definitions on the chalkboard.

minority	group of people who make up less than half of the total population
autonomy	self-governing
compact	occupying a small area

   Discuss how each term relates to the student classroom population. (The number of people who have a horse might be in the *minority*; when groups get together to work, they do so in a modified state of *autonomy*; closet space might be *compact*, etc.)

2. Distribute a copy of page 107 to each student. As a class or in small groups, have the students access the focus Web site and complete the activity page.

3. Review the vocabulary words from step 1. Now have the students share how the terms relate to their study of China's culture. Distribute a large sheet of drawing paper to the students. They fold the paper twice to make three sections and then write one term in each section and illustrate its meaning.

4. As a class, revisit the **Culture and Ethnic** link and select the links to take you to visit **Chen Song, Chinese Traditional Artist,** and **Chinese Historic Relics**. On the backside of their vocabulary papers or on separate sheets of drawing paper, have the students write brief summaries of an item of interest and then illustrate their words.

THE CHINESE CULTURE

Name ____

Launch this Web site: http://www.chinatoday.com

Directions: Select the link "Culture and Ethnic." Read about the Chinese culture and complete the answers on this page.

Ethnic Groups

1. Which ethnic group numbers the greatest in China? ______________________

2. How many ethnic groups are represented altogether in China? ______________________

3. Tell where the Han and minority groups live. ______________________

____

____

Spoken and Written Languages

4. Why did the government have to help devise a standardized written language for certain ethnic groups in China? ______________________

____

____

National Regional Autonomy

5. What is a national regional autonomous country? ______________________

____

____

6. Why do you think the government is divided this way? ______________________

____

7. Why is the government aiding the minority nationality areas? ______________________

____

8. What do the minorities do in return? ______________________

____

CHINA (cont.)

Extended Activities:

- Display a country map of China. Have the students take turns reviewing the map to identify any major cities, points of interest, or general geography information. Divide the class into nine groups to re-access the focus Web site to select the **Travel and Tourism** link and then choose **Tourist Hot Spots**. Assign the groups a different "hot spot" to access. (See listing below.) They write what it is and draw a picture of it on a three-by-five-inch note card. Then each group shares the information about its "hot spot" and tapes the card to the appropriate location on the map (north, south, central, etc.).

Hainan Island	Forbidden City	Temple of Heaven
Huangshan Mountain	Shanghai	Terra-cotta Army
The Great Wall	Hong Kong	Tiananmen Square

- Introduce students to the Chinese art of paper cutting by first visiting this site to view some actual cuts and then designing and creating their own.

  Chinese Paper Cuts
  http://www.isaacnet.com/culture/papercut.htm

  To make a paper cut, each student will need a sheet of black and a sheet of white construction paper. The students fold the white paper and make several random cuts to remove small pieces of the paper. When they are done cutting, they mount the white paper onto the black paper. If desired, the students may trim the black paper to match the outline of the white paper.

- *The Year of the Boar and Jackie Robinson* by Bette Bao Lord is a story that tells of one young Chinese girl's confusion as she struggles to adjust to American culture and society. Share this story with the class. Upon its completion, visit this Web site about the Chinese zodiac and see if events from the story matched the boar's personality. Students may also wish to spend some time discovering their own Chinese zodiac animals. Chances are most students were born during the same two consecutive years. Students may access the information by themselves, or you may wish to access the Web site as a class.

  Welcome to the Chinese Zodiac!
  http://www.xmission.com/~ericward/zodiac/index.html

GREECE

Objective:

Ancient civilizations enter the high-tech world with these activities about the Greek culture. Students first learn about the science of archaeology, measuring time in centuries, and the Byzantine Empire; then they go online to learn about some important archaeological finds in and around Athens and consider their importance to discovering more about the Greek culture.

Materials Needed:

- chalkboard
- one copy of page 111 for each student
- writing paper

Focus Web Site—Destination URLs:

Embassy of Greece
http://www.greekembassy.org/

About This Site: The ancient world has modernized itself with this interactive Web site about Greek culture and society. Select from one of eleven category links and then choose the topic of interest. Each Web page has bountiful graphics and graphic and text links to provide entertaining information about Greece.

Alternative Web Sites:

Greek Civilization Home Page
http://www-adm.pdx.edu/user/sinq/greekciv/carr.html

InfoGreece
http://www.infogreece.com/

Greece: The Complete Reference
http://38.244.258.2/TRAVEL/

Map of Greece (graphic only)
http://www.lib.utexas.edu/Libs/PCL/Map_collection/europe/Greece.GIF

GREECE (cont.)

Pre-Internet Activity:

Lead a discussion about archaeology. Post the term on the board and have the students share what they know about it. Then explain that archaeology is the study of past cultures and peoples through their remains and relics. Discuss the kinds of things archaeologists look for and the places they might dig. Also have students reflect on the importance and purpose of this science. Explain to the students that they will visit the ancient city of Athens, Greece, to learn about some archaeological finds and places to go to see the relics and ruins.

Teaching the Lesson:

1. Discuss how to measure time using *centuries*. Explain that a century is a measure of 100 years and that the century number is always one hundred ahead of the actual year. For example, the year 1946 (19 being the number in the hundreds) is in the 20th century. Post these years on the chalkboard and have the students tell which century they were in.

   1278 1476 1868 932 75

   Then post these centuries and have the students tell a year from that century.

   16th century 12th century 8th century 32nd century

2. Next discuss the *Byzantine Empire* if the students are unfamiliar with this term. Explain that the Byzantine was the eastern half of the Roman Empire beginning in 395 A.D. Greece became part of the Byzantine Empire after the fall of the Roman Empire. Its capital was Constantinople (now Istanbul).

3. Distribute a copy of page 111 to each student. As a class, visit the Web site and complete the page.

4. After reading about the ruins and artifacts, discuss how these items led archaeologists to learn about the Greek culture. Have the students consider the excitement of the finds and write journal entries as if they were archaeologists on an important dig in Greece and have just unearthed a new relic.

Extended Activities:

- Visit an archaeological site each day of your study of Greece. From the **Greek Culture** link, select the **Athens/Piraeus** link and then **Archaeological sites**. Start with the first site on the first day, read the information and look at the pictures, and then select from the remaining eleven links, visiting a different one each day.

- From the *Embassy of Greece* home page, select the **General Information** link and then **History of Greece**. Students can read a brief history of this land and link to terms for which they would like more information. Have small groups of students write about an important event. Combine the groups' phrases to make a time line of Greece's history.

SITES TO SEE FROM GREECE'S PAST

Name____

Launch this Web site: http://www.greekembassy.org/

Directions: Select the **Greek Culture** link. Then click on the **Culture map** of Greece. Find the city of **Athens** on the map and click on it. Now follow the links below to read about some ancient ruins turned tourist attractions and how they relate to the Greek culture.

Use the map key to find and click on Archaeological site **A 13** to visit Theagenes' Spring at Megara.

1. In what year do archaeologists believe this fountain was built? ______________________

2. What was this structure used for? ______________________

   Click the <**Back**> arrow from the task bar. Use the map key to find and click on Museum 7 to visit the Archaeological Museum of Eleusis.

3. Why was this museum built? ______________________

   ____

4. What is the Eleusis amphora? ______________________

   ____

   What is pictured on its neck? ______________________

   ____

   What is pictured on its side? ______________________

   ____

   Click the <**Back**> arrow from the task bar. Use the map key to find and click on the Byzantine site **B1** to visit the Kaisariani Monastery.

5. Which way from Athens is this monastery? ______________________

   ____

6. What decorates the walls inside the church? ______________________

   ____

RUSSIA

Objective:

Students will come to appreciate the democratic society in which they live after reading a century-long tale of life in communist Russia. The students follow an abbreviated time line through Russian history as they match events to the dates of their occurrence.

Materials Needed:

- chalkboard
- one copy of page 114 for each student
- yellow and red crayons

Focus Web Site—Destination URLs:

The Russian Chronicles
http://www.f8.com/FP/Russia/RCtoc.html

About This Site: Journey through Russia with people who know what landmarks to look for and the questions to ask. Visit famous sites and tourist attractions as well as getting a feel for the personalities and attitudes of the Russian people through interviews and personal accounts of the past.

Alternative Web Sites:

A Brief Visit to Russia
http://www.midwinter.com/~koreth/russia/

Russia on the Web
http://www.valley.net/~transnat/

RUSSIA *(cont.)*

Pre-Internet Activity:

Discuss the type of government people in the United States enjoy. (democracy) Have the students list some attributes about this type of government. Then review some other types of governments. (See the list below.) Discuss the differences among the governments and have the students list some pros and cons of living in both democratic and dictatorship societies. Explain that they will have a chance to visit a Web site to learn about the history of Russia of a century ago to the fall of communism that occurred in recent history by following one family's story as the family struggled to survive while living in Russia.

Democratic Governments—ruled by the populous

- constitutional monarchy—king or queen acts as figurehead, has minimal (if any) power
- republic—ruled by elected officials

Dictatorship Governments—ruled by one person or one body of people

- Fascism—people exist to serve the state
- Communism— all economy and land is controlled by the government

Teaching the Lesson:

1. Review the concepts of decades (periods of ten years) and centuries (periods of one hundred years). Demonstrate with the example of the year 1967. We say this year was "in the 60s" and the 20th century. (See step 1 from page 110 for additional information regarding centuries.) List some years at random on the chalkboard and have the students tell the decade and century.
2. Give a brief overview of the history of Russia. (See below.)
3. Distribute a copy of page 114 to each student. As a class or in small groups, have them access the Web site and complete the activity page.
4. As a class, have the students figure out how much time elapsed between Russia and Germany's Non-Aggression Pact and the German invasion of Russia. (*about two years*)
5. Have the students color-code the sentences to indicate joyful and peaceful times and difficult and fearful times in Russian history according to the family's accounts. The students use a yellow crayon to indicate happy eras and a red crayon to indicate sad eras. When finished, review the emotions the family endured as Russian inhabitants. How do they think it would compare to an American's experience through the same century? Why?

A Brief History of the Russian Government

Up until 1917, Russia was ruled by a royal family; the king or emperor was called a tsar, and the queen or empress was called the tsarina. The tsars ruled similarly to the English royal family in that they had complete rule over the country. In 1917 the tsar abdicated and was eventually replaced by the Communist Party (first led by Lenin). This continued until 1991 with the fall of communism and the breakup of the Soviet Union.

A CENTURY OF UNREST

Name ____

Launch this Web site: http://www.f8.com/FP/Russia/RCtoc.html

Directions: Click the **Road Stories** link and then **100 Years of Revolution**. Follow the **<Continued>** and **<Next>** links to read about one family's experience in Russia over the past century. Match the years to the events that took place during that time.

1. The Treaty of Brest Litovsk may have ended Russia's involvement in WWI, but a civil war was just beginning.	1905
2. Lenin became the leader of the new Soviet Union.	1914
3. A revolution was brewing with unrest and labor strikes meant to protest the tsarist government.	1918
4. Russia entered World War I.	1920s
5. This decade brought fear and paranoia to Russia's people with unwarranted arrests, encampments, and shootings.	1930s
6. The Nazis attacked Russia.	1939
7. The Nazis announced their surrender to end WWII.	June 22, 1941
8. Russia entered a Non-Aggression Pact with Hitler.	May 9, 1945
9. A Russian cosmonaut orbited the Earth.	1956
10. Nikita Khrushchev made a "secret speech" to the 20th Party Congress, denouncing Stalin and what he stood for. This began Russia's "thaw."	1961
11. The USSR dissolved with Gorbachev's resignation.	1985
12. Mikhail Gorbachev came to power.	1991

Thematic Topics

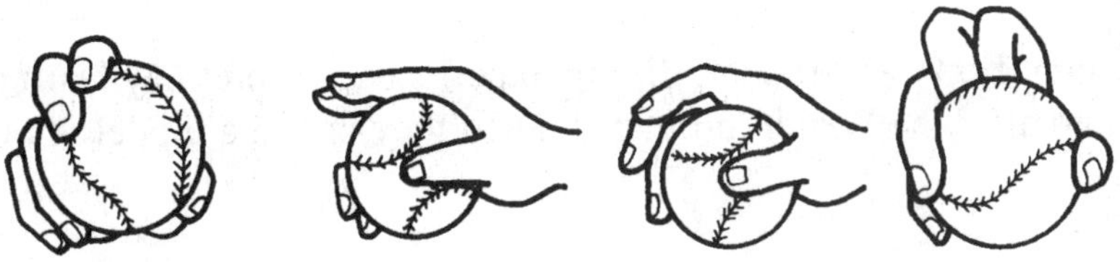

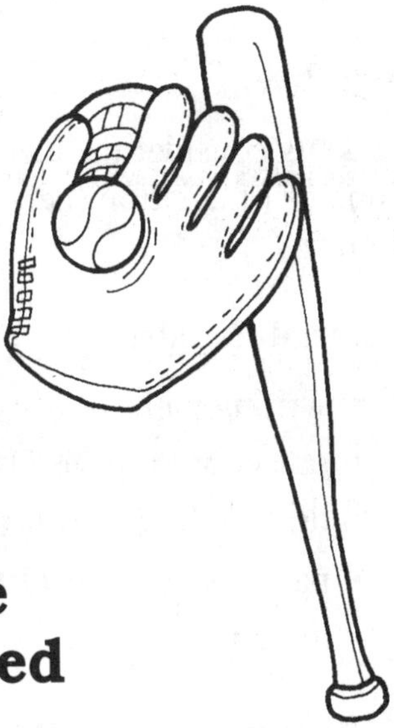

Bring these themes new life with Internet activities focused on the following topics:

The History of Aviation

Amelia Earhart
Charles Lindbergh

Baseball

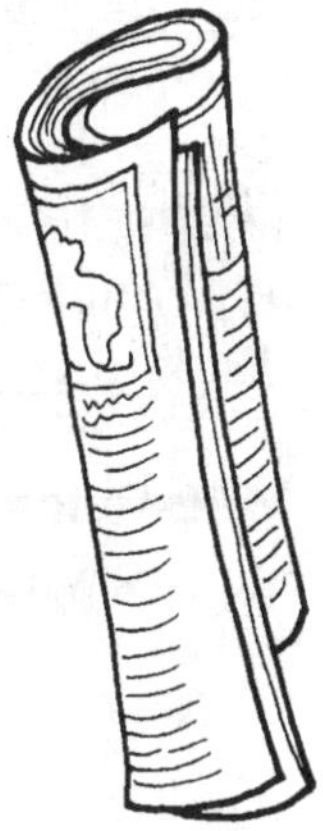

Current Events

The Olympics

The Vikings

THE HISTORY OF AVIATION

Objective:

Students consider the elements of flight and modern flying experiences before they learn about the pioneers of aviation (before and after the Wright brothers). Then they create a model of an early aircraft.

Materials Needed:

- writing paper
- one copy of page 118 for each student
- drawing paper or tagboard
- patterns on page 119
- thread

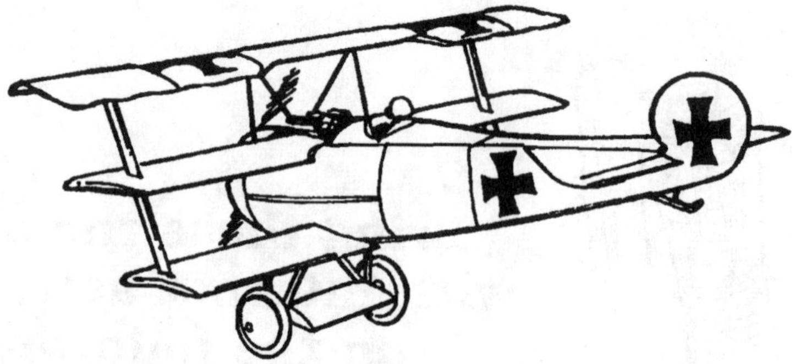

Focus Web Site—Destination URLs:

Aviation History OnLine Museum
http://www.aviation-history.com/

About This Site: Seven links related to the history of aviation provide students with information and photos of early engineers, inventors, and aircraft, beginning in the late 1800s.

Alternative Web Sites:

"To Fly Is Everything..." A Virtual Museum Covering the Invention of the Airplane
http://hawaii.cogsci.uiuc.edu/invent/airplanes.html
(Link to the **Tale of the Airplane** or the **Inventor's Gallery**.)

Flights to Reality
http://muttley.ucdavis.edu/Book/instructor.html
(Link to **History**.)

Milestones of Flight Gallery 100 (by the Smithsonian Institution)
http://www.nasm.edu/GALLERIES/GAL100/gal100.html

THE HISTORY OF AVIATION *(cont.)*

Pre-Internet Activity:

Take a walk outside. Have the students sit quietly and observe birds in flight. (Students may also make observations through the window.) They consider and jot down all the scientific factors that come into play when a bird flies through the air (e.g., wind speed and direction, gravity, wing span, weight of the bird, etc.). Place the students into groups of four or five to share their ideas with their classmates. As a class, students share ideas that everyone seems to have in common as well as a few unique individual ideas members of their group share. Explain that although we take airplanes and flight (aviation) for granted now, in the days when this was a new field, many people experimented with different aircraft in trial-and-error attempts to be the first to "fly."

Teaching the Lesson:

1. Have the students share any flying experiences they may have had: the foods they were served, using the facilities, the kind of seats, other surroundings, etc. Ask the class whether they think these surroundings are comfortable. Explain that the men who first attempted to fly did so usually standing up or suspended in air. No stewardesses came to take their lunch orders nor did they have handy airsick bags and bathrooms. Not that they needed them; the first flights lasted mere seconds. Tell the students that they will have a chance to learn about three men who were the earliest, but not always successful, pioneers in the field of aviation.

2. Distribute a copy of page 118 to each student. As a class or in small groups, access the focus Web site and complete the activity page.

3. Have the class consider the similarities and differences of the attitudes and techniques among the three aviation pioneers listed on the sheet.

4. Airplanes improved dramatically and rapidly as the world entered the 20th century. Have the students work in pairs to re-access the focus Web site and link to **Historic Aircraft**. They select a plane to view and jot down its name, manufacturer, and country of origin as well as a brief synopsis of its history and a sketch detailing its shape and adornments. Students then use drawing paper or heavy tagboard to cut and glue a model of the plane and color or paint its markings. (The patterns on page 119 may be helpful if the plane has a similar body style. If not, the students may use the patterns as guides to create their models.) They share their planes and information with the class. Attach a length of thread to the tops of the planes and suspend them from the ceiling.

Extended Activity:

Invite an aviation expert from a local or international airport to come to your class and further discuss the history of aviation and how advances in this field affected American society.

PIONEERS OF THE SKY

Name ____

Launch this Web site: http://www.aviation-history.com/

Directions: The Wright brothers weren't the only ones on a mission to invent the airplane. Several men helped them achieve success by laying the groundwork for this exciting "new" field—aviation. First link to **The Early Years**. Then link to read about these three men and answer the questions.

1896—Otto Lilienthal—Germany

1. Describe Lilienthal's philosophy toward aviation engineering. ____________________

____

____

2. Draw a person in the glider to show the position in which Lilienthal flew his gliders.

1903—Samuel Pierpont Langley—USA

3. What did Langley call his flying machines? ____________________

4. How did his first flight in October, 1903, turn out? ____________________

____

1906—Santos Dumont—France/Brazil

5. What is unique about the manner in which one flew Dumont's aircraft? ____________________

____

____

THE HISTORY OF AVIATION *(cont.)*

Use these patterns with step 4 from page 117.

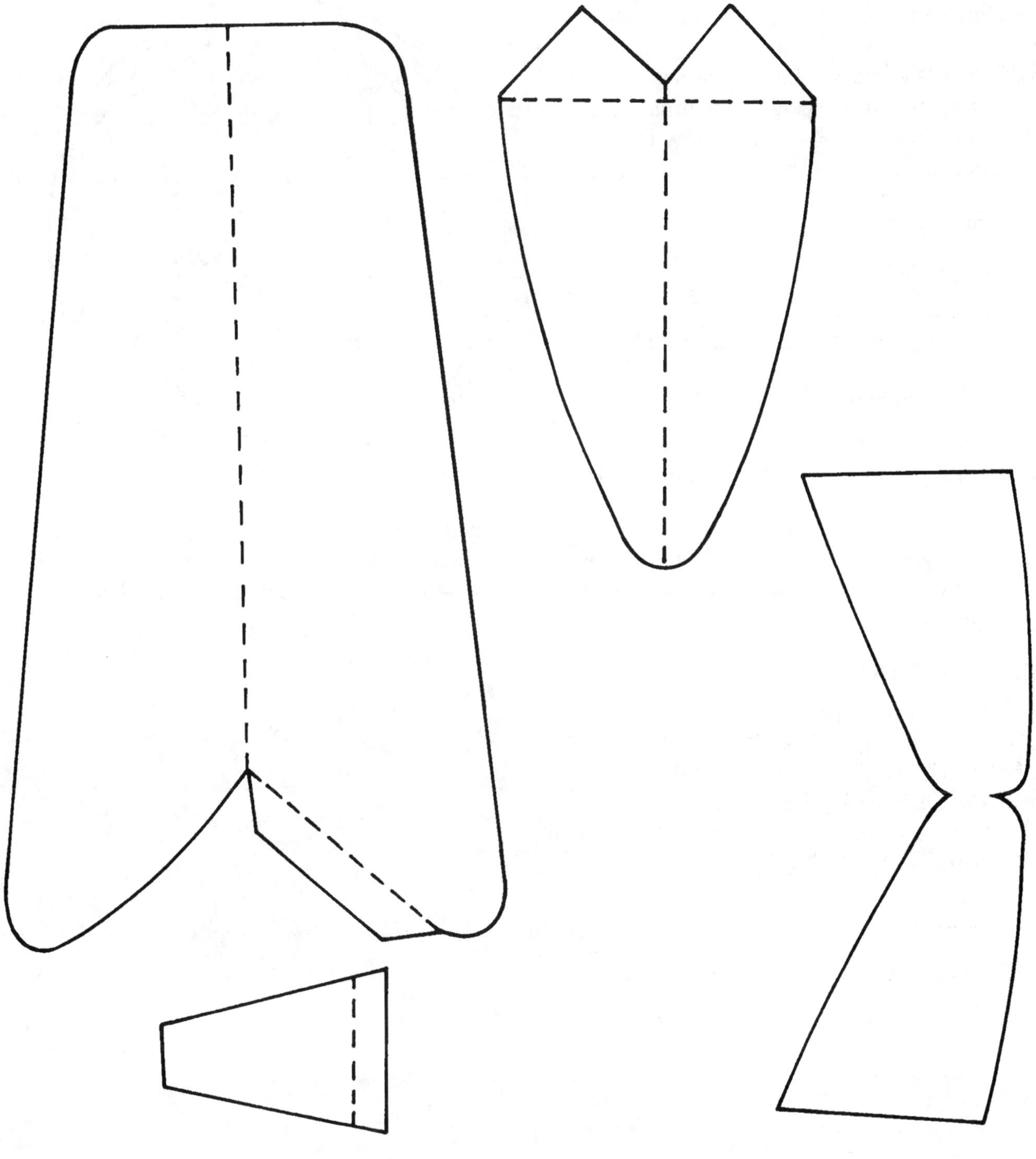

THE HISTORY OF AVIATION: AMELIA EARHART

Objective:

Students travel the world with Amelia Earhart, mapping out their own route and then comparing it to the one she flew as she attempted to circle the earth in an airplane. Students also learn and apply military time as it pertained to Earhart's disappearance.

Materials Needed:

- world map
- chalkboard
- one copy of page 122 for each student

Focus Web Site—Destination URLs:

Amelia Earhart
http://www.ionet/~jellenc/eae_intr.html

About This Site: This site takes viewers from Earhart's years as a youngster through the traumatic experience of her final flight as she attempted to fly around the world. Accompanying pictures and quotes draw students' attention to the enlarged text and add to the overall value of this site.

Alternative Web Sites:

World Flight 1997
http://worldflight.org/

The Earhart Project
http://www.tighar.org/Projects/AEdescr.html

THE HISTORY OF AVIATION: AMELIA EARHART *(cont.)*

Pre-Internet Activity:

On a world map, have the students determine the shortest possible route if they were to travel around the world, beginning in their hometown, circling the globe, and returning to their hometown. (Explain that the students can travel only up to 2,000 miles at a time.) Would they travel east around the Earth or west? How long would they expect this journey to last? What would be some possible dangers in attempting this excursion? Explain that Amelia Earhart attempted to achieve this goal but disappeared over the Pacific Ocean while she was on the last leg of her journey. The students will read on the Internet more about her flight and the controversy her disappearance stirred.

Teaching the Lesson:

1. Lead a discussion about military time. (*Every time has two hour positions and two minute positions. Hours are counted similarly to civilian time from one second after midnight until 12 noon—12 hundred hours. Then the hours continue counting up until 12 midnight—24 hundred hours. To read afternoon civilian time, subtract 12 from the hour position.*) Write several military times on the chalkboard and have students determine the civilian time. Students should also practice determining how much time has elapsed between two military times.

   Military Time Examples:

   04:56 = 4:56 A.M. 15:30 = 3:30 P.M.

   10:25 = 10:25 A.M. 20:05 = 8:05 P.M.

2. Distribute a copy of page 122 to each student. As a class or working in small groups, have the students access the focus Web site and complete the activity page.

3. As a class, follow Earhart's flight stops around the world. Compare her pattern to those the students mapped out in the pre-Internet activity.

   ❶ Los Angeles, CA, to Miami, FL
   ❷ to San Juan, Puerto Rico
   ❸ to the northeast edge of South America
   ❹ to Africa
   ❺ to the Red Sea
   ❻ to Karachi, Pakistan
   ❼ to Rangoon, Burma
   ❽ to Bangkok, Thailand
   ❾ to Singapore, Malaysia
   ❿ to Port Darwin, Australia
   ⓫ to Bandung, Indonesia
   ⓬ to Lae, New Guinea
   ⓭ toward the Howard Islands

Extended Activity:

Have the students consider the theories to explain Earhart's disappearance. They select one of these theories or think of one of their own to write a legend explaining Earhart's disappearance. Combine them to create a book, "Where Are You, Amelia Earhart?"

AMELIA EARHART'S FINAL FLIGHT

Name ____

Launch this Web site: http://www.ionet/~jellenc/eae_intr.html

Directions: Link to "The Last Flight." Read about Earhart's attempt to fly around the world. Answer the questions below.

1. Why did Amelia Earhart alter her flight plan? ______________________________

   ____

2. In which U.S. state did her flight begin? ______________________________

3. What was the date? ______________________________

4. Describe Earhart's attitude toward this flight. ______________________________

   ____

5. About how much time had elapsed between her departure from California and the day she attempted to make it back to California over the Pacific Ocean? ____________________

   ____

6. How much time had elapsed between her last transmission and the time they determined her flight must have gone down?

   Time of last transmission: ____________________

   Time determined flight was down: ____________________

   Total time: ____________________

7. Read the theories that explained Earhart's disappearance. Which seems the most believable? ____

   ____

   Which seems the least believable? ______________________________

   ____

THE HISTORY OF AVIATION: CHARLES LINDBERGH

Objective:

Students consider the motivation Lindbergh had for attempting to fly solo, nonstop over the Atlantic Ocean. Then they access the Internet to gather clues to discover his hometown.

Materials Needed:

- one copy of page 125 for each student
- U.S. map or U.S. desktop maps

Focus Web Site—Destination URLs:

Get Real!: Pit Stop: Charles Lindbergh
http://www.wpt.org/getreal!/400/402/LINDY/LINDY.HTM

About This Site: Tantalizing questions with suitable hints lead students to learn about Charles Lindbergh. Large text and accompanying photos make this site student-friendly and a must-visit for aviation enthusiasts.

Alternative Web Sites:

Friendship Flight '97
http://www.friendshipflight.com/
(Link to <u>**About Lindbergh**</u> or <u>**The Flight**</u>.)

Charles A. Lindbergh
http://www.broonale.co.uk/ukraine/lindbergh.html

The Untold Story of the Spirit of St. Louis
http://www.erols.com/ryannyp/

The Spirit of Lindbergh
http://ice.ucdavis.edu/~robyn/lindbergh.html

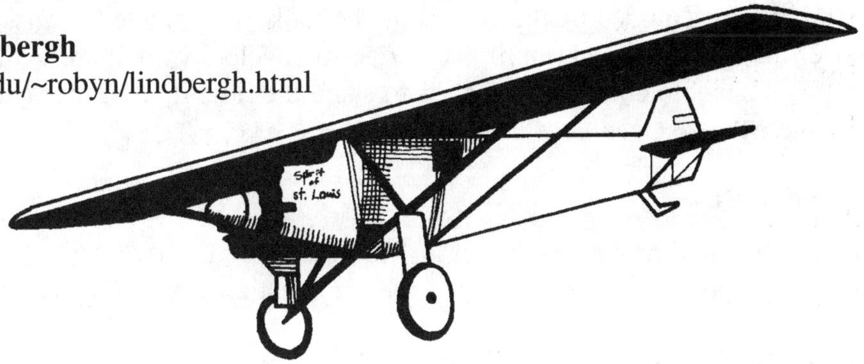

THE HISTORY OF AVIATION: CHARLES LINDBERGH (cont.)

Pre-Internet Activity:

Lead a discussion about what motivates people to do things that have never been accomplished before. What would the students be willing to do for $25.00? Explain that Lindbergh attempted to be the first person to complete a solo, nonstop flight over the Atlantic Ocean when airplanes and aviation were still fairly new concepts. Have the class brainstorm the hazards and dangers that he might have faced and how he might have prepared for his flight. Then explain that he did it to win a $25.00 prize. Was this prize money worth the effort? Of course, his success brought more than prize money. Overnight (literally), Lindbergh became a famous hero. How does this label add to the glory of his accomplishment?

Teaching the Lesson:

1. Explain to the students that they will visit a Web site to learn more about Lindbergh while they simultaneously try to solve the answer to the riddle, *Where is Charles Lindbergh's hometown?*

2. Distribute a copy of page 125 to each student. Display a U.S. map or allow students to use individual desk maps. Launch the Web site with the class. Read the first section and have the students use the map to make predictions about the location of Lindbergh's hometown.

3. Continue reading the information, gathering clues as well as information to answer the questions on the activity page.

4. Finish reading to discover the answer to the puzzling question (*Little Falls, MN*). The students find his hometown on the map. If it's not identified, have them use a Minnesota map. Were the clues enough to help the students solve the riddle? What other clues could the creators of this Web site have given?

5. (Optional) Help the students use the legend on a world map to measure the distance between New York and Paris. Divided by the 33½ hours he took to complete his mission, the students will discover his average speed (mph). How does this velocity compare with modern flights? Invite a local travel agent to come to your class to share the time it takes to travel from one city to another across the Atlantic Ocean.

Extended Activities:

- Have the students write a newspaper article describing Lindbergh's achievement and landing in Paris. They should include answers to the six question words, *who*, *what*, *where*, *when*, *how*, and *why*.

- Have the students make up riddles about other famous people's hometowns. Students write their clues on note cards. Collect the cards and play "Where was I born?" Students may use desktop maps and almanacs to follow the clues and solve the riddles.

"LUCKY LINDY"

Name ____

Launch this Web site: http://www.wpt.org/getreal!/400/402/LINDY/LINDY.HTM

Directions: Read the first section of information. See if you can figure out Charles Lindbergh's hometown. Continue reading and answer the questions.

1. Where was Charles Lindbergh born? ______________________________

2. Where did he go to college? ______________________________

3. From where did he take off on his historic flight across the Atlantic ocean?______________________________

   ____

4. Where did he land 33 1/2 hours later? ______________________________

5. What was his motivation for attempting this feat? ______________________________

   ____

6. Why did he take so few provisions? ______________________________

   ____

7. How did he stay awake for the entire flight?______________________________

   ____

8. How did Lindbergh earn his nickname? ______________________________

   ____

9. What was Lindbergh interested in when he was growing up? ______________________________

   ____

10. How do you think his interest applied to his achievement? ______________________________

    ____

BASEBALL

Objective:

Students get in the baseball spirit with a rousing rendition of "Take Me Out to the Ball Game." Then they select a favorite team to investigate in regards to their league and divisional affiliations and current standings.

Materials Needed:

- lyrics to song for students to view (see page 127)
- one copy of page 128 for each student
- calculators

Focus Web Site—Destination URLs:

The Official Site of Major League Baseball
http://www.majorleaguebaseball.com/

About This Site: For all the latest sports scores and information, this site will satisfy any baseball fan. The links are well organized and the information is up-to-date and ready for access.

Alternative Web Sites:

ESPN SportsZone
http://ESPN.SportsZone.com/mlb/

Yahoo! Sports: [Your Team Name]
http://www.yahoo.com
(Type in the team's location and name encased in quotation marks and click <**Search**>. Select a Web site suitable to your needs.

OR to select from a list of teams from the Yahoo! database, follow these steps.

Go to the Yahoo! search engine at www.yahoo.com. Type in Baseball and click <**Search**>. Select the category link **Recreation: Sports: Baseball: MajorLeague Baseball (MLB)**. Select the **Teams** topic to search a list of major league teams.

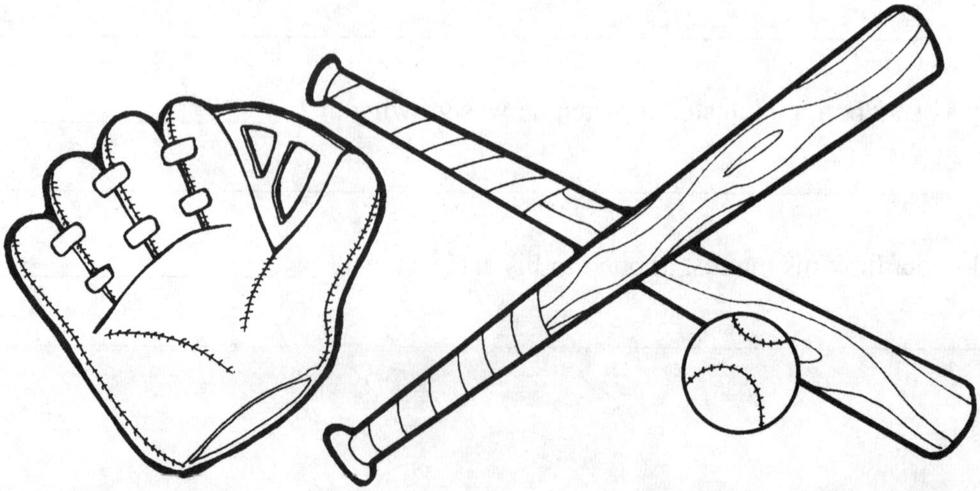

BASEBALL *(cont.)*

Pre-Internet Activity:

Ask the students if they know which sport holds the honor of being considered "America's Favorite Pastime"? After revealing that it is baseball, teach the students the song "Take Me Out to the Ball Game." (Ask your music teacher to provide a recording of the tune.)

"Take Me Out to the Ball Game"

Take me out to the ball game,
Take me out to the crowd.
Buy me some peanuts and crackerjacks,
I don't care if I ever get back.
So it's root, root, root for the home team,
If they don't win it's a shame.
Cuz it's ONE! TWO! THREE! Strikes you're out
At the old ball game!

Teaching the Lesson:

1. Explain to the class that they will be working with a partner to discover the current standings (wins and losses) of their favorite major league baseball team. Have the students get with a partner and decide on a team to reference. Assign students a team if they have no favorite. Record the students' names and teams on a sheet of paper.

2. Discuss the division of the major leagues. (*They are divided into two leagues, the American and National. Each league is divided into divisions. Each team is affiliated with a league and division. Although now teams play any other team, regardless of league or division, they essentially are competing against teams in their own league and division for a chance to attend the World Series.*)

3. Distribute a copy of page 128 to each pair of students. As a class, demonstrate how to go about moving around the links to find the information listed on the activity sheet. Use a team no one has chosen. Then allow the teams to access the Web site on their own.

4. Discuss how the students' teams are doing in their divisional standings. Explain that the students can calculate the teams' winning percentage by adding the wins and losses and then dividing the wins by the total number of games.

   Example:

Team: Detroit Tigers	Wins: 17	Losses: 8	Total: 25 games
Winning percentage:	17 ÷ 25 = .68 or 68%		

OUT AT THE BALL PARK

Name ____

Launch this Web site: http://www.majorleaguebaseball.com/

Directions: Link to either the American League (AL) or the National League (NL). Select a team to reference. Follow the links to complete the information.

① Click on the **NL** or **AL Standings** link to find out the wins and losses for all the teams in each league.

② Click the team name's link to find out the manager's name and view the team emblem.

③ Click the **Playing Info** link for information about the team's home field.

Team (location and name) ______________________________________

League and division ______________________________________

Manager ______________________________________

Ball field ______________________________________

List all the teams in this division.
Fill in the standings for each team.

Team	**Wins**	**Losses**
____________________	_____	_____
____________________	_____	_____
____________________	_____	_____
____________________	_____	_____
____________________	_____	_____
____________________	_____	_____
____________________	_____	_____

Draw the team's emblem.

BASEBALL *(cont.)*

Extended Activities:

- Have the students create a banner of the team they referenced. They fold a 12-by-18 inch sheet of drawing paper in half lengthwise and then cut from the two corners of one side to the end of the fold line to form a triangular banner. They color the banner in the team's colors and include the emblem from the activity page. Post them on a bulletin board entitled "Baseball Fanatics!"

- Have the pairs return to the focus Web site and team pages and then select the **Franchise History** link. Here the students will find a thorough history of how their team came into existence. They take notes, writing down an abbreviated history, and then share their information with the class.

- Each ball field is unique in design, architecture, and dimensions. Because of the great variety of playing fields, each stadium also has its own set of "ground rules" to which visiting teams must adhere. Have the partners re-access the focus Web site and their team's Web pages and select the **Playing Info** link. They read the situations and ground rules unique to their team's home field and then report to the class. List the statements on a sheet of chart paper. Then compare the fields. Are any two stadiums more similar or different than others?

- Die-hard sports fans will be eager for the latest sports news. Students will be even more apt to read the sports section when they are the focus of the headlines! Have the students access the ESPN SportZone Web site (see **Alternative Web Sites** on page 126) and select an article of interest to them. They record the who, what, where, when, why, and how of the article, then use this same information to rewrite the article while substituting their own name for the star player. Have the students type the new articles in a word processing or desktop publishing program in newspaper layout. Cut and paste the articles on a 30-by-23-inch sheet of butcher paper folded to 15 by 30 inches to resemble a newspaper. Place the resulting "child star" sports page in the reading corner for students to browse in their free time.

- If the history of baseball better suits your curriculum, don't miss these fascinating Web sites specifically created to tell all.

  Total Baseball
  http://www.totalbaseball.com/

  Negro Leagues Professional Baseball
  http://www.majorleaguebaseball.com/nbl/

  Legendary Ladies of Baseball
  http://members.aol.com/legendlady/index.html

CURRENT EVENTS

Objective:

News reporters make live broadcasts seem easy and effortless. But it takes a great deal of training and practice to become a respected news reporter. Students find out firsthand what reporting the news is like as they practice their summarizing and vocal skills.

Materials Needed:

- weekly newspapers
- one copy of page 132 for each pair of students
- large piece of cardboard and paints (for a "play" television for the classroom)
- camcorder and videotape

Focus Web Site—Destination URLs:

Yahooligans! search engine home page
http://www.yahooligans.com

About This Site: Students select a topic (**The Scoop**) from the search engine home page and then link to any one of several news-related links.

Alternative Web Sites:

Jeremy's News Page
http://ucsu.colorado.edu/~robinsjr/News.html

News of the Weird
http://www.nine.org/notw/notw.html

This Is True
http://www.thisistrue.com/

CURRENT EVENTS *(cont.)*

Pre-Internet Activity:

Assign students the task of watching the evening news at home. They discuss with their parents the details of one of the stories that interests them and then they write a one-paragraph summary of the story of interest. Allow time for the students to share their reports with the class. Discuss, also, the manner in which the reporter communicated the story: *What was her attitude? How was she dressed? Where did she stand? In which direction did she face? Did her face give away any hints as to how she felt about the story?* etc. Explain that each student will have a chance to gather the latest "scoop" off the Internet and report the news to the class in a professional manner like a real-life news reporter.

Teaching the Lesson:

1. Assign students news partners. They will have the same partners throughout the school year. Each week, have the class scan the headlines for interesting news items. Set aside fifteen minutes for the students to share what's going on in the world that interests them and discuss the stories. In addition, allow a different pair each week to go online to obtain a news story to share with the class.

2. Each pair needs a copy of page 132. Write one of the following category links on the line entitled "Today's news category."

Current Events	Newswires
International	Television
Newspapers	Weather
News Magazines @	

   (If possible, assign seven pairs each week to link to each of the categories above.) After clicking the link, students have a list of Web sites from which to choose. They select a site that appeals to them, link to it, and then get the scoop!

3. Allow the pairs about fifteen minutes of class time to organize their story and write a dialog for the class. They may wish to conduct an interview, do an on-scene report, or simply report the news like an anchor at the station.

4. Create a television screen for the students to stand behind with paints and a piece of cardboard from the side of a large box. The students give their news report, live and on television, on Friday mornings.

5. Another option is to videorecord the students giving their news stories and broadcast it on Friday's morning show if your school conducts one. Record all the students' stories on one tape and show it to the parents at Open House or another parent function toward the end of the school year.

ROVING REPORTER

Name ____

Launch this Web site: http://www.yahooligans.com

Directions: As a reporter, your job is to report the news accurately and in an interesting fashion to earn the respect of your audience. Discover what's current in the news by linking to **The Scoop** and then the category listed below. Read an interesting story, record the information, and then report to your classmates to fill them in.

Today's news category ____

Title of the news article ____

Who was involved ____

Where it took place ____

When it happened ____

What it was about ____

Why it's important news ____

How it affects us ____

Details: ____

____

____

____

____

____

____

____

____

____

THE OLYMPICS

Objective:

Let the games begin! Students apply their math skills to calculate the number of years ago the first Olympics began as well as the number of years they lasted. They begin to consider differences between the ancient and modern games in the classroom and then go online to learn more differences as well as reading about actual ancient Olympians.

Materials Needed:

- calculators (optional)
- one copy of page 135 for each student

Focus Web Site—Destination URLs:

The Ancient Olympics
http://olympics.tufts.edu/

About This Site: Go back in time (way back in time) to the first Olympic events. Select from seven related links to investigate the manner in which the games of then compare to the modern Olympic games, including a guided tour of the original site of the Olympics.

Alternative Web Sites:

The Ancient Olympic Games Virtual Museum
http://devlab.dartmouth.edu/olympic/

First Olympic Games—Athens 1896
http://orama.com/athens1896/

Olympic Golden Nuggets
http://www.cam.org/~fishon1/olympic.html

Author's Note: The men who competed in the ancient games did so without clothing. Some of the graphics (mostly etchings, carvings, or cartoons) reveal the Olympians from a front or side view. Use discretion when accessing these sites with students.

THE OLYMPICS *(cont.)*

Pre-Internet Activity:

Lead a discussion about the students' favorite Olympic sports and competitors. Ask them to identify the location of the most recent Olympic games. Explain that the Olympics began in Greece in 776 B.C. Ask the students to recall the prizes the winners received. Explain that early victors were awarded head wreaths made of olive tree branches. The students then recall some sports of the modern Olympic games. Explain that the very first Olympics had only one running event but soon included numerous running events and other sports. Tell the students that they will have a chance to further investigate the differences between the ancient and modern Olympic games on the Internet as well as read about an actual ancient Olympian.

Teaching the Lesson:

1. Help the students discover how many years ago the first Olympics took place. Then they consider all the advancements and changes the world has witnessed throughout that time. Besides the above-mentioned comparisons, how else do the students think the ancient Olympics differed from the modern games?

2. Explain that the ancient Olympics ended around 394 A.D. Help the students discover the duration of the ancient Olympics. (*1,170 years*) Explain that in this amount of time, many changes took place in the games. They will compare this period of time known as the "ancient" Olympics to the "modern" games which date back to 1896, only a little over one hundred years ago.

3. Distribute a copy of page 135 to each student. If desired, launch the Web site as a class and link to **Ancient and Modern Olympic Sports**. Read the information there and have the students complete numbers 1, 2, and 3 on their sheets.

4. Divide the class into five groups and assign each team to access one of the five ancient Olympians listed at the **Stories** link, or have the students work with a partner to access this link and select an Olympian of their choice. Have the students share their research with the class.

Olympic Background Information

- The Greek calendar was based on the Olympiad (four-year interval between games).
- Hercules founded the games.
- Temples and statues were erected to honor Zeus.
- The games were canceled during WWI (1916) and WWII (1940 and 1944).
- In 1992, the winter and summer games began alternating every two years.

THE ANCIENT OLYMPIC GAMES

Name ____

Launch this Web site: http://olympics.tufts.edu/

Directions: The original Olympics were very different from the events the world celebrates in modern times. Read about how they were different by selecting the link "Ancient and Modern Olympic Sports." List three ways the ancient Olympics were different from the modern games.

Ancient Games	Modern Games
1. ____________________	____________________
____________________	____________________
2. ____________________	____________________
____________________	____________________
3. ____________________	____________________
____________________	____________________

Click the **Stories** link. Select one of the names of an ancient Olympian. Read his story and then complete the information below.

His name ____

His sport ____

Year(s) he participated ______________________________________

How he became an Olympian ___________________________________

____

____

____

____

____

____

____

THE OLYMPICS *(cont.)*

Extended Activities:

- Visit the FAQ link and copy the list of 10 frequently asked questions about the Olympics. Post them on the chalkboard or on chart paper. Have the students speculate about the correct answers and then access the focus Web site as a class to link to the answers.

- Have a small group of students apply their Internet research skills to discover where the next three Olympic games (summer and winter) will be held. (*At the time of composition, the next two sites are 2000 (summer) in Sydney, Australia and 2002 (winter) in Salt Lake City, UT. 2004 and 2006 are as yet undecided.*)

- Besides a little bit of history, students can learn about some Olympic ceremony protocol at the third alternative Web site listed on page 133. As a class, launch this Web site and link to **the Olympic Oath**. Have a volunteer read the oath to the class. Discuss the purpose of this or any oath. What does it mean to take an oath? Who else takes an oath? (*doctors, witnesses, the President, etc.*) Have the students work with a partner to write a classroom oath. To what will they pledge their word? Post them all for the class to read and consider the words before starting each day.

- Linking to the **Origin of the Rings** from the same site above will take students to a Web page full of information about the Olympic flag. Have them consider the Olympic motto and how it applies to athletes as well as everyday activities.

- Hold a mini-Olympics in your classroom. Have small groups of students work together to create an opening ceremony performance lasting between two and three minutes in length. Some ideas include jumping rope, juggling, dancing, flag waving, etc. Then assign each student a country to represent in the Olympic games. (Depending on the number of students, you may have as few as four or as many as eight countries. Each country should have five to eight representatives.) Each person must participate in a different event from his or her teammates. Following are some ideas for events and how winners are determined. Keep track of the first, second, and third place winners. Make gold, silver, and bronze medals from construction paper and attach them to a length of yarn for the students to place over their necks during the awards ceremonies following the games.

straw javelin (distance)	running long-jump (distance)
cotton ball shot put (distance)	string hurdles (time)
running races (time)	crab-walk soccer (score)
Frisbee™ discus (distance)	basketball shots (count)

- Check out this site listing interesting tidbits about the Olympic games, mascots, torches, Olympic firsts, and frequently asked questions.

  Olympics FAQ on the Web
  http://www..andrew.cmu.edu/~mmdg/Almanac/

THE VIKINGS

Objective:

Who pirated, marauded, stole, and still managed to find time to explore the Americas? Why, the Vikings, of course! Students get a glimpse into the life of these feared seamen as they learn about the history of the Vikings and some Viking lore. Then the students try their own play on words; instead of "going a-viking," will students "go a-literaring"?

Materials Needed:

- world map or globe
- one copy of page 139 for each student
- writing paper

Focus Web Site—Destination URLs:

Viking Voyage 1000
http://www.viking1000.org/

About This Site: Read up on a modern-day re-creation of the voyages of the Vikings. Students link to **Viking Lore** to glimpse a brief history of these fearless heathens and learn a little bit about their culture.

Alternative Web Sites:

The Viking Network
http://viking.no/

World of the Vikings
http://www.pastforward.co.uk/

THE VIKINGS *(cont.)*

Pre-Internet Activity:

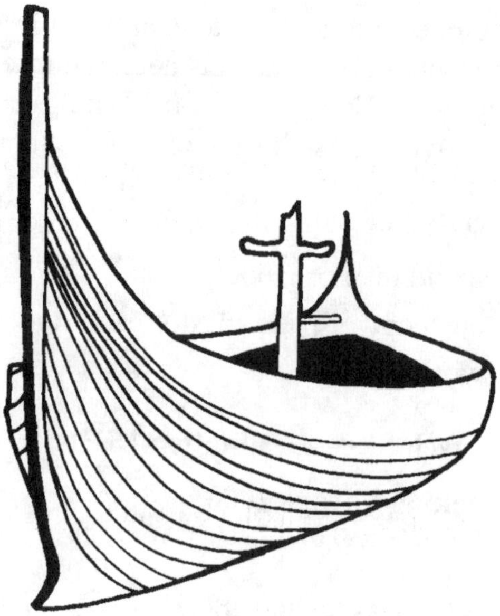

Explain to the students that long before Columbus made his historic voyage to the Americas, the Vikings had already been here and left, although they were known to have explored areas much farther north from where Columbus sailed. Originally, the Vikings set out from Scandinavia (Norway, Denmark, and Sweden) to conquer lands such as France, England, and northern Russia, to name a few. Some settled in Iceland; Eric the Red settled a colony in Greenland. They sailed all over and were known for their fierce bravery and uncompromising attacks. Show students the locations of the countries from which they sailed on a world map or globe. Then follow water routes to show the countries to which they traveled in search of riches. Explain to the students that they will have a chance to learn more about the Vikings on the Internet.

Teaching the Lesson:

1. The Vikings were known for their ruthless pursuit of wealth; they would do anything to get it and have no second thoughts about killing those who stood in their way. Explain that the Vikings are said to have been *pagans* or *heathens* because of their totally remorseless behaviors. Later Vikings began "practicing" Christian faiths, but their behaviors didn't change in the slightest.

2. Distribute a copy of page 139 to each student. Assist the students in logging onto the Internet, reading the information and answering the questions.

3. Explain that the terms *Vikings* and *Norsemen* tend to be used interchangeably. Norsemen were the people who lived in Scandinavia. The Norsemen who raided and pillaged were called Vikings (*Vik* meaning "harbor" or "bay"). When they went out on raids, they were said to be "going a-viking." Have the class work in small groups to come up with a term to use to describe events that occur during the school day.

   Example: reading might become "going a-literaring" or "going a-booking"

   Other possible daily activities:

lunch	grammar	erasing the board
recess	computers	sharpening pencils
math	snack	coloring
science	cleaning up	turning in work
social studies	listening	dismissal

THE VICTORIOUS VIKINGS

Name ____

Launch this Web site: http://www.viking1000.org/

Directions: Click on the graphic to enter the Viking world. From the large circle of Viking links, click on "Viking Lore." Read the information and answer the questions.

1. Why did Leif Ericson leave Greenland? ______________________________

   ____

2. In what year did he set sail? ______________________________

3. Who was his father?______________________________

4. How were women of Viking voyages treated? ______________________________

   ____

5. Why didn't the Vikings stay in North America?______________________________

   ____

6. How did the Vikings share their adventures? ______________________________

   ____

7. How many letters made up the Viking alphabet? ______________________________

8. Why did most letters in the Viking alphabet have straight lines?______________________________

   ____

9. How did the Vikings celebrate bravery? ______________________________

   ____

10. Why are Viking etchings found all over the world? ______________________________

    ____

INTERNET PERMISSION SLIP AND AWARD

Dear Parents,

We are fortunate to provide the most current electronic resources for our students. With your permission, our class will be exploring the Internet to gather valuable information related to various topics throughout the year. Please note that we will not be visiting "chat" rooms. All of the Internet sites have been previewed and deemed suitable for young learners. Each Internet activity will be supervised by an adult. At no time will the students be allowed to have free access to the Internet.

Please sign this form granting permission for your child to use Internet resources and return it to school. We welcome you to join us one day to experience this extraordinary opportunity (days and times to be determined). Thank you for supporting our efforts to provide the most exciting educational opportunity for our students!

Sincerely,

_______ I give my child, ________________________________, permission to work on the Internet.

_______ I DO NOT wish for my child to work on the Internet.

Signed:________________________________

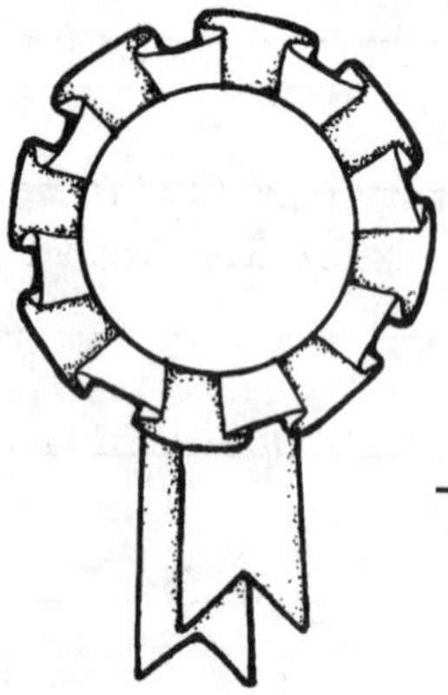

Congratulations!

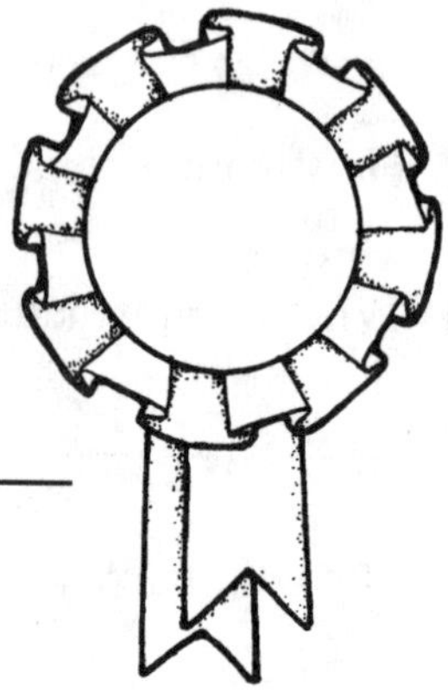

This Award Is to Certify That

____

Is an Internet Wizard!

Signed:________________________________

Date:________________________________

GLOSSARY OF INTERNET TERMS

Chat	Live electronic typing conversation among a group of people
Domain	Name of the server through which a Web site comes to the viewer
E-mail	Electronic messages sent and received across the Internet
FAQ	Acronym for *frequently asked questions*
Home Page	First Web page for a particular Web site
HTML	Acronym for *Hypertext Markup Language*
Internet	Electronic resource of electronic networks used to provide information via an Internet service provider and Web browser
ISP	The acronym for *Internet service provider* (e.g., *America Online, CompuServe*, or local Internet access point)
Link	Point at which a viewer may jump from one Web page to another; may be within the same Web site or connect to a different Web site
Log on	The act of dialing into an ISP and gaining access to the Internet through a server
Modem	Electronic equipment that allows the computer to access the Internet through a telephone line
Search Engine	Tool with which a viewer may search for Web sites about specific topics and/or information (e.g., *Yahoo!, Infoseek, Alta Vista*)
Server	Specially networked computer that is always linked to the Internet
URL	Acronym for a Web site's *Uniform Resource Locator*; think of this as the Web site's address; when typed in and searched, the Web browser takes the viewer directly to the site with this code
Web Browser	Tool which allows the Internet user to view Web pages (e.g., *Netscape, Microsoft Internet Explorer*)
Web Page	Specific page on the Internet
Web Site	A group of related Web pages within a particular domain or access area
WWW	Acronym for the *World Wide Web*

ANSWER KEY

Page 14 Pirates

1. check students' answers
2. whipping or flogging
3. captain or quartermaster
4. man overboard, marooning, dunking

Page 22 Alexander Graham Bell

1. deaf
2. Edinburgh, Scotland
3. make sound visible
4. phonoautograph
5. speak words
6. telephone
7. March 10, 1876; "Mr. Watson, come here, I want you!"

Page 26 George W. Carver

1. 1860, 1861, 1864; unrecorded births
2. 12; check students' answers
3. develop industrial application from farm products
4. any 3: peanuts, sweet potatoes, pecans, soybeans
5. any 2: rubber substitute, dyes, pigments, paints, stains
6. accept any reasonable response
7. check students' lists

Page 29 Thomas Alva Edison

1. F	6. F	10. T
2. F	7. T	11. T
3. T	8. F	12. T
4. T	9. T	13. F
5. T		

Page 37 The Morse Invention

1. Samuel Finley Morse; 1840s
2. long and short pulses
3. check students' drawings
4. Alfred Vail
5. undersea
6. Continental or International Code

Page 37 The Morse Invention *(cont.)*

7. any 4: telegrams, railroads, Associated Press, industry, Civil War, oil
8. automated teleprinter
9. True

Page 40 Famous First Flight

1. Wilbur
2. toy helicopter
3. Neither finished high school.
4. printers
5. bicycle
6. The Smithsonian Institution
7. lift, propulsion, control
8. yaw, pitch, roll
9. kite
10. Orville; Dec. 10, 1903; 12 seconds

Page 48 Susan B. Anthony

1. dining room
2. front parlor
3. Mary's bedroom
4. third-floor study
5. study
6. back parlor
7. Susan's bedroom

Page 51 Albert Einstein

1. violin
2. boring, intimidating
3. no
4. high school math and physics
5. patent examiner
6. Berlin
7. his cousin, Elsa
8. solar eclipse
9. Zionism, world peace
10. warn of Germany's A-bomb

Page 58 Rosa Parks

1. not giving up a bus seat
2. accept any reasonable response
3. first act towards equality for minorities
4. minorities had no civil rights
5. rallied others to demand equality
6. others would follow her
7. bus boycotts, overrule of ordinance, outlaw segregation
8. founding of the Rosa and Raymond Parks Institute for Self-Development, served on staff of U.S. Representatives
9. accept any reasonable response
10. Montgomery, Tuskegee, Pine Level

Page 62 Jackie Robinson

1. any four: won a batting title, led the league in stolen bases, played in an All-Star Game, played in the World Series won MVP award, elected to the Hall of Fame
2. any two: racist manager, racist opponents, hateful fan mail
3. refused to accept segregation; helped integrate hotels and restaurants.
4. stadium at UCLA named after him, Jackie Robinson Award
5. football, basketball, track
6. no African Americans allowed to play in the NBA or NFL
7. accept any reasonable response

Page 72 U.S. Geography

1. 30 N; 81 W
2. 42 N; 83 W
3. 37 N; 97 W
4. 40 N; 78 W
5. 40 N; 111 W
(check students' maps)

ANSWER KEY *(cont.)*

Page 88 Westward in a Wagon

check student's labels

1. 10 ft.; 4 ft.; 2 ft.
2. 1,300 lbs.
3. to keep the rain out
4. any four; water barrel, butter churn, shovel, axe, feed trough, chicken coop
5. milk cows, mules

Page 92 Calfornia Gold Country

(in order from top to bottom) 6 (7/48) 8 (8/8/48), 3 (1/24/48), 10 (2/28/49), 1 (1812), 7 (7/18/49), 9 (12/5/48), 4 (3/15/48), 5 (5/29/48), 2 (1842)

Page 99 On Safari in Okavango

1. Botswana
2. summer rains from Angola flow to the Okavango River to Botswana
3. about 25 miles
4. about 60 miles
5. about 125 miles check student's drawings

Page 103 The Great Land of Canada

1. Hong Kong, India, Philippines, Taiwan, China
2. check students' labels
3. U.S.A., United Kingdom, Japan
4. U.S.A., United Kingdom, France

Page 107 The Chinese Culture

1. Han
2. 56
3. Han—all over, 4 compact communities; Minorities—60% total land area, mostly at border regions
4. Many minority nationalities had no written language.

Page 111 Sites to See from Greece's Past

1. 500 B.C.
2. fetching water
3. to house relics from the digs
4. vase; blinding of a cyclops, myth of Perseus and the Gorgons
5. east
6. paintings

Page 114 A Century of Unrest

1. 1918	7. May 9, 1945
2. 1920s	8. 1939
3. 1905	9. 1961
4. 1914	10. 1956
5. 1930s	11. 1991
6. June 22, 1941	12. 1985

Page 118 Pioneers of the Sky

1. get up in the air to get a "feel" for the airplane before attaching an engine
2. check students' drawings
3. aerodromes
4. crashed in a river
5. standing up; pilot controlled the plane

Page 122 Amelia Earhart's Final Flight

1. safer due to weather conditions
2. California
3. May 21, 1937
4. would be her last; hoped it would be successful
5. one month, 12 days (about 1 1/2 months)
6. 20:14; 21:30; 1:16
7. check students' answers

Page 125 "Lucky Lindy"

1. Detroit, MI
2. University of Wisconsin
3. New York
4. Paris, France
5. $25 prize
6. fuel weighed too much
7. held his eyes open
8. no one had achieved this act before
9. mechanics, airplanes
10. check students' answers

Page 139 The Victorious Vikings

1. search for more wooded and fertile land
2. 1000
3. Eric the Red
4. as equals
5. run off by natives
6. storytelling
7. 16
8. easy to inscribe
9. erected stone memorials with pictures and words
10. widely sailed

RESOURCES AND BIBLIOGRAPHY

Software

Compton's Interactive Encyclopedia, Version 4.0., 1996 Edition. (1995). Compton's NewMedia, Inc.

WebWhacker Version 2.0. The ForeFront Group, Inc., 1996. 1330 Post Oak Boulevard, Suite 1300, Houston, Texas, 77056. Internet: http://www.ffg.com

Online Services

America Online (800) 827-6364

CompuServ (800) 848-8990

Microsoft Internet Explorer

Netscape (415) 254-1900

Net Search Providers

Alta Vista http://www.altavista.com/

Excite http:www.excite.com/

Infoseek http://www.infoseek.com/NS

Yahoo! http://www.yahoo.com

Yahooligans! http://www.yahooligans.com

Literature

Classroom Connect. "Copyright and the World Wide Web," pages 8 and 9. Volume 3, Number 5. February 1997.

Comparing Regions. Silver, Burdett and Ginn, 1995.

Haag, Tim. ***Internet for Kids***. Teacher Created Materials, Inc., 1996.

Lord, Bette Bao. ***In the Year of the Boar and Jackie Robinson.*** Harper & Row, Publishers, 1984.

PC Novice Guide to the Web. Peed Corporation, 1996.

Polly, Jean Armour. ***The Internet Yellow Pages: Special Edition.*** Osborne McGraw-Hill, 1996.

Tweedle, Dominic. ***Growing Up in Viking Times.*** Troll Associates, 1994.